Urban America

IN THE TWENTIETH CENTURY

Crowell Source Readers in American History

DAVID BRODY, *General Editor*

The purpose of this series is to provide students of American history with a means for approaching key problems through the evaluation of the historical evidence. Each of the volumes in the series concentrates on several major issues relating to one area of American history. The editors have chosen documents that focus on those issues in an immediate way and from a variety of contemporary standpoints. Each section contains a solid body of evidence for the study of the topic being covered. Introductory essays that set the issues in their historical context are included in each volume and each section is preceded by a headnote that relates each document to the theme of the section. The objective of this series will be fulfilled if the student is enabled to think independently about the issues contained in these volumes. The titles in the series are *American Foreign Relations in the Twentieth Century*, edited by Manfred Jonas; *American Thought in the Twentieth Century*, edited by David Van Tassel; *The American South in the Twentieth Century*, edited by Robert L. Brandfon; *Industrial America in the Twentieth Century*, edited by David Brody; *Urban America in the Twentieth Century*, edited by Milton D. Speizman; and, forthcoming, *American Politics in the Twentieth Century*, edited by John Braeman.

B. Axelrod

Urban America

IN THE TWENTIETH CENTURY

Documents Selected and Edited by

MILTON D. SPEIZMAN

Tulane University

Thomas Y. Crowell Company / *New York* / *Established 1834*

 / Library of Congress Catalog Card Number: 68-13386 / Series design by Laurel Wagner / Manufactured in the United States of America

For MY MOTHER AND FATHER

Preface

So completely has general American history become American urban history that the matter of selection of readings for a book of this nature becomes a rather personal one. The limits on the study of the city are rapidly disappearing. It was, therefore, necessary to sample a bit here and there in many areas, among them politics, housing, economics, and the theater. If these choices entice the reader into consulting the longer original works, my purposes will have been met.

To attempt to thank everyone who has helped me prepare this volume would be hopeless and dangerous, dangerous because of the inevitability of momentarily forgetting the important assistance someone has provided. My gratitude for the contribution of my wife, Arleen Florence Speizman, however, is far from the conventional and must be avowed, for in a sense she had been working with me on this book long before its genesis. Her actual part in its preparation has been both practical and supportive beyond measure. And, finally, a word for our daughter, Elissa Ruth Speizman, who was old enough to give help and not too old to be beyond offering it.

M.D.S.

Contents

Introduction

By the turn of the nineteenth century the trend was unmistakable: the United States was changing into a nation of cities. That vast continental expanse which had been an assurance to Jefferson of the permanent dominance of a virtuous agrarian people was fast becoming a mere setting for the urban jewels, precious or tawdry. During the preceding four decades the urban population had nearly quintupled, while the rural population had failed even to double itself. Put another way, Americans living in cities had, in 1860, formed only nineteen per cent of the total population; in 1900 they were thirty-nine per cent.

The sources of this urban flood were both domestic and foreign. Men and women, often young, discouraged by the drudgery, tedium, and frequent failure of farm life so graphically revealed by Hamlin Garland, turned to the city. There they hoped to find wider opportunities in the burgeoning industry and business of the postwar years; there living itself promised to be much more exciting. As the origins of immigration shifted from northern and western Europe to the southern and eastern regions of that continent, the newcomers, too, responded to the call of industry, to the vision of golden pavements. Furthermore, the new immigrants tended to be too poor to take up farm lands of their own, or to be completely inexperienced in the techniques of the newer machine-oriented agriculture. The city was their choice, if, indeed, they even recognized any other.

With the dawn of the new century came the reluctant recognition that the city had become a permanent feature of the American landscape. And what was seen was not always very pretty. James Bryce's observation in 1888 that "the government of cities is the conspicuous failure of the United States" remained for many, perhaps most, urban places an apt reproach. So widespread was municipal corruption that an occasional honest mayor, like "Golden Rule" Jones of Toledo or Tom Johnson of Cleveland, was a curiosity. The inevitable tie between corrupt government and corrupt business had created some of the worst urban slums in the western world. Investigations notwithstanding, a widely extensive movement for eradicating the slums did not appear as it had in much of Europe. Proponents of changing the dismal scene were striving mightily to gather support for their programs, which ranged from model cities to revolutionary socialism. Social workers tried with some success to soften the effects of urban evils through a variety of devices. And even in the most densely populated sections of the cities a vitality was surging which could not be suppressed, a vitality which was often contrasted with the sameness of rural life.

As the Progressive movement reached its climax in the second decade of the century, American political and social problems, largely centered in the cities, were at last receiving full, if reluctant, attention. National party platforms, notably in 1912, gave full consideration to the difficulties of the cities and their populations. A variety of devices and programs were proposed and tried, among them city manager and commission government, civil service reform, and Socialist administrations. In the effort to learn exactly what the urban situation was, the social survey became institutionalized; indeed, the pioneers of such studies, in Pittsburgh, founded a magazine named simply *The Survey*. The First World War brought new wealth and opportunity to the city, but with it new problems or aggravations of older ones. Fearful race riots disgraced some of the communities which had called Negroes from the South to tend the machines producing the goods of war.

The influx of Southern Negroes was not, however, reversible, and great centers of Negro life were established in many northern cities with results which appeared to be both ominous and hopeful. In the generally euphoric 1920's, hope seemed to be more plausible than despair. The tide of municipal reform was still advancing, despite occasional setbacks; city governments were turning their attention to such matters as public recreation programs. Business was in the saddle as never before; the businessman was the hero of American life and the arbiter of its mores and beliefs. The radicals continued to find fault with the reign of Babbitt, but they gained few listeners; the public found the outrages of Chicago's gangsters more absorbing. Only the architects and city planners managed to locate an audience for their warnings of unbridled and unplanned urban growth, but that audience was polite rather than convinced.

The bubble burst late in 1929, and the next three years were ones of despair. Millions of men and women found themselves without means of earning a livelihood, and a welfare system designed to provide for a small number of unemployables failed to meet the needs of mass unemployment. A few of the jobless turned to radical proposals, but most waited despondently for prosperity to turn the corner. City administrations tried harder than other levels of government to provide for the needy, but by late 1932 many were virtually bankrupt, for their efforts to provide relief were complicated by a burdensome system of overlapping local governments inherited from a rural past and no longer appropriate to urban needs.

The only recourse remaining was the national government. In 1933 the new administration of Franklin D. Roosevelt faced the challenge. From emergency cash relief payments to work programs, through relief agencies and public works, the New Dealers managed to lift the pall of hopelessness which lay over much of the nation. Their vision lay beyond relief and recovery: they sought to raise all segments of the population and all sections to new levels. Though complete recovery evaded Roosevelt and his followers until the coming of the Second World War, the voters, particularly those in the cities, were convinced that in this President they had a leader who cared for them. And they elected him again and again, as it turned out, for life.

The war ended the Great Depression and brought a period of prosperity unequaled in coverage and duration. With the coming of peace, millions of white and blue collar workers moved beyond the old city limits to found those series of suburbs sometimes called "Megalopolis." Their places in the old core areas were taken by new arrivals from rural districts, especially by Southern Negroes. The Northern ghetto became a commonplace. Downtowns deteriorated, the cities grew uglier, the air was polluted. Appeals to inaugurate an era of quality were largely ignored. Again, as in the 1930's, it appeared that only the active intervention of the federal government could save the cities. A possible beginning was made in 1965 when Congress, after refusing to do so in the past, approved the creation of a Department of Housing and Urban Development. This legislation was indeed only one of a series of measures adopted by Congress, which was anxious to deal with serious urban problems. Urban Redevelopment, the "War on Poverty," efforts to deal with pollution of air and water, and the Model Cities Demonstration Program were important examples of Administration and Congressional efforts. If the nation was willing to devote effort and money for many years, the American city might yet become a place of beauty, of health, of culture, where men "remain together in order to live the good life."

Urban history, someone has said, has become merely a synonym for social history. If true, this is one more bit of evidence that Americans, indeed citizens of all "developed" nations and those who would be like them, have become so thoroughly urbanized that rural problems have assumed secondary importance. Some Americans still proclaim the values of the bucolic life, but few return to those allegedly virtuous pastures. American history has become the history of the cities and their peoples. Only in the cities can there be that gathering of artists and craftsmen, thinkers and builders that can bring fulfillment to mankind in the twentieth century and beyond.

MANNAHATTA

I was asking for something specific and perfect for my city,
Whereupon lo! upsprang the aboriginal name.

Now I see what there is in a name, a word, liquid, sane, unruly, musical, self-sufficient,
I see that the word of my city is that word from of old,
Because I see that word nested in nests of water-bays, superb,
Rich, hemm'd thick all around with sailships and steamships, an island sixteen miles long, solid-founded,
Numberless crowded streets, high growths of iron, slender, strong, light, splendidly uprising toward clear skies,
Tides swift and ample, well-loved by me, toward sundown,
The flowing sea-currents, the little islands, larger adjoining islands, the heights, the villas,
The countless masts, the white shore-steamers, the lighters, the ferry-boats, the black sea-steamers well-model'd,
The down-town streets, the jobbers' houses of business, the houses of business of the ship-merchants and money-brokers, the river-streets,
Immigrants arriving, fifteen or twenty thousand in a week,
The carts hauling goods, the manly race of drivers of horses, the brown-faced sailors,

The summer air, the bright sun shining, and the sailing clouds aloft,
The winter snows, the sleigh-bells, the broken ice in the river, passing along up or down with the flood-tide or ebb-tide,
The mechanics of the city, the masters, well-form'd, beautiful-faced, looking you straight in the eyes,
Trottoirs throng'd, vehicles, Broadway, the women, the shops and shows,

SOURCE: Walt Whitman, *Leaves of Grass* (New York and London: D. Appleton & Company, 1910), pp. 360–61.

A million people—manners free and superb—open voices—hospitality—the most courageous and friendly young men,
City of hurried and sparkling waters! city of spires and masts!
City nested in bays! my city!

PART I

The City Observed

THE city burst upon the American consciousness at the beginning of the century as a mass of problems—as it has remained to this day. The most obvious fact about the city was the ineptness and, indeed, corruption of its government. Chiefly responsible for arousing public curiosity and indignation at this widespread condition was the band of able journalists dubbed "muckrakers" by President Theodore Roosevelt. In city after city they found the public, not merely supine, but acquiescent in the dominance of thievish bosses (Selection 1).

As New York's corruption was the most notorious, so the Empire City's housing was the worst, perhaps, in the entire Western World. The early decades of the century was the era of the survey; one of the most famous was devoted to a detailed exposure of the slums which had shocked Jacob Riis a decade earlier (Selection 2).

Suggestions for dealing with the urban crisis were plentiful, ranging from Socialism (Selection 3) to beautification (Selection 4). Less ambitious were the efforts of some church leaders and social workers who hoped, through the institutional church and the social settlement, to alleviate some of the distress and quickly to turn the immigrants who populated the slums into Americans (Selection 5).

The city, however, was not all evil and despondency; if it had been it might not have lasted. In the midst of the slums there could be found hope, gaiety, and creativity (Selection 6). And whatever its drawbacks, few would seriously consider exchanging the teeming city for bucolic peace (Selection 7).

1 / A MUCKRAKER'S WARNING

In 1903 the dean of muckrakers, Lincoln Steffens, feared that Americans really did not care enough about honest government to keep it when they had it.

Just about the time this article will appear, Greater New York will be holding a local election on what has come to be a national question: good government. No doubt there will be other "issues." At this writing (September 15th) the candidates were not named nor the platforms written, but the regular politicians hate the main issue, and they have a pretty trick of confusing the honest mind and splitting the honest vote by raising "local issues" which would settle themselves under prolonged honest government. So, too, there will probably be some talk about the effect this election might have upon the next presidential election; another clever fraud which seldom fails to work to the advantage of rings and grafters, and to the humiliation and despair of good citizenship. We have nothing to do with these deceptions. They may count in New York, they may determine the result, but let them. They are common moves in the corruptionist's game and, therefore, fair tests of citizenship, for honesty is not the sole qualification for an honest voter; intelligence has to play a part, too, and a little intelligence would defeat all such tricks. Anyhow, they cannot disturb us. I am writing too far ahead, and my readers, for the most part, will be reading too far away to

SOURCE: Lincoln Steffens, "New York: Good Government in Danger," *McClure's Magazine,* XXII (November, 1903), 84–92.

know or care anything about them. We can grasp firmly the essential issues involved and then watch with equanimity the returns for the answer, plain yes or no, which New York will give to the only questions that concern us all:

Do we Americans really want good government? Do we know it when we see it? Are we capable of that sustained good citizenship which alone can make democracy a success? Or, to save our pride, one other: Is the New York way the right road to permanent reform?

For New York has a good government, or, to be more precise, it has a good administration. It is not a question there of turning the rascals out and putting the honest men into their places. The honest men are in, and this election is to decide whether they are to be kept in, which is a very different matter. Any people is capable of rising in wrath to overthrow bad rulers. . . . New York has done it several times. With fresh and present outrages to avenge, particular villains to punish, and the mob sense of common anger to excite, it is an emotional gratification to go out with the crowd and "smash something." This is nothing but revolt, and even monarchies have uprisings to the credit of their subjects. But revolt is not reform, and one revolutionary administration is not good government. That we free Americans are capable of such assertions of our sovereign power, we have proven; our lynchers are demonstrating it every day. That we can go forth singly also, and, without passion, with nothing but mild approval and dull duty to impel us, vote intelligently to sustain a fairly good municipal government, remains to be shown. And that is what New York has the chance to show; New York, the leading exponent of the great American anti-bad government movement for good government.

According to this, the standard course of municipal reform, the politicians are permitted to organize a party on national lines, take over the government, corrupt and deceive the people and run things for the private profit of the boss and his ring, till the corruption becomes rampant and a scandal. Then the reformers combine the opposition: the corrupt and unsatisfied minority, the disgruntled groups of the majority, the reform organizations;

they nominate a mixed ticket, headed by a "good business man" for mayor, make a "hot campaign" against the government with "Stop thief" for the cry, and make a "clean sweep." Usually, this effects only the disciplining of the reckless grafters and the improvement of the graft system of corrupt government. The good mayor turns out to be weak or foolish or "not so good." The politicians "come it over him," as they did over the business mayors who followed the "Gas Ring" revolt in Philadelphia, or the people become disgusted as they did with Mayor Strong, who was carried into office by the anti-Tammany rebellion in New York after the Lexow exposures. Philadelphia gave up after its disappointment, and that is what most cities do. . . .

. . . . .

The administration of Mayor Seth Low may not have been perfect, not in the best European sense: not expert, not coordinated, certainly not wise. Nevertheless, for an American city, it has been not only honest but able, undeniably one of the best in the whole country. Some of the departments have been dishonest; others have been so inefficient that they made the whole administration ridiculous. But what of that? Corruption also is clumsy and makes absurd mistakes when it is new and untrained. The "oaths" and ceremonies and much of the boodling of the St. Louis ring seemed laughable to my corrupt friends in Philadelphia and Tammany Hall, and New York's own Tweed regime was "no joke," only because it was so general, and so expensive —to New York. It took time to perfect the "Philadelphia plan" of misgovernment, and it took time to educate Croker and develop his Tammany Hall. It will take time to evolve masters of the (in America) unstudied art of municipal government—time and demand. So far there has been no market for municipal experts in this country. All we are clamoring for to-day in our meek, weak-hearted way, is that mean, rudimentary virtue miscalled "common honesty." Do we really want it? . . .

. . . . .

. . . The New York way is on trial, for New York has what the whole country has been looking for in all municipal crises—

the non-political ruler. Mr. Low's very faults, which I have emphasized for the purpose, emphasize the point. They make it impossible for him to be a politician even if he should wish to be. As for his selfishness, his lack of tact, his coldness—these are of no consequence. He has done his duty all the better for them. Admit that he is uninteresting; what does that matter? He has served the city. Will the city not vote for him because it does not like the way he smiles? Absurd as it sounds, that is what all I have heard against Low amounts to. But to reduce the situation to a further absurdity, let us eliminate altogether the personality of Mr. Low. Let us suppose he has no smile, no courtesy, no dignity, no efficiency, no personality at all; suppose he were an It and had not given New York a good administration, but had only honestly tried. What then?

Tammany Hall? That is the alternative. The Tammany politicians see it just as clear as that, and they are not in the habit of deceiving themselves. They say "it is a Tammany year," "Tammany's turn." They say it and they believe it. They study the people, and they know it is all a matter of citizenship; they admit that they cannot win unless a goodly part of the independent vote goes to them; and still they say they can beat Mr. Low or any other man the anti-Tammany forces may nominate. So we are safe in eliminating Mr. Low and reducing the issue to plain Tammany.

Tammany is bad government; not inefficient, but dishonest; not a party, not a delusion and a snare, hardly known by its party name—Democracy; having little standing in the national councils of the party and caring little for influence outside of the city. Tammany is Tammany, the embodiment of corruption. All the world knows and all the world may know what it is and what it is after. For hypocrisy is not a Tammany vice. Tammany is for Tammany, and the Tammany men say so. Other rings proclaim lies and make pretensions, other rogues talk about the tariff and imperialism. Tammany is honestly dishonest. Time and time again, in private and in public, the leaders, big and little, have said they are out for themselves and their own; not for the public, but for "me and my friends"; not for New York, but for Tammany. Richard Croker said under oath once that he worked for his own pockets all the time, and Tom Grady, the Tammany orator, has brought his crowds to their feet cheering sentiments as primitive, stated with candor as brutal.

The man from Mars would say that such an organization, so self-confessed, could not be very dangerous to an intelligent people. Foreigners marvel at it and at us, and even Americans—Pennsylvanians, for example—cannot understand why we New Yorkers regard Tammany as so formidable. I think I can explain it. . . .

. . . . .

Tammany's democratic corruption rests upon the corruption of the people, the plain people, and there lies its great significance; its grafting system is one in which more individuals share than any I have studied. The people themselves get very little; they come cheap, but they are interested. Divided into districts, the organization subdivides them into precincts or neighborhoods, and their sovereign power, in the form of votes, is bought up by kindness and petty privileges. They are forced to a surrender, when necessary, by intimidation, but the leader and his captains have their hold because they take care of their own. They speak pleasant words, smile friendly smiles, notice the baby, give picnics up the River or the Sound, or a slap on the back; find jobs, most of them at the city's expense, but they have also news-stands, peddling privileges, railroad and other business places to dispense; they permit violations of the law, and, if a man has broken the law without permission, see him through the court. Though a blow in the face is as readily given as a shake of the hand, Tammany kindness is real kindness, and will go far, remember long, and take infinite trouble for a friend. . . .

. . . . .

As a New Yorker, I fear [Charles F.] Murphy [new Tammany boss] will prove sagacious enough to do just that: stop the scandals, put all the graft in the hands of a few tried and true men, and give the city what it would call good government. Murphy says he will nominate for mayor a man so "good" that his goodness will astonish New York. I don't fear a bad Tammany mayor; I dread the election of a good one. . . .

. . . . .

New York has gone on fighting, advancing and retreating, for thirty years till now it has achieved the beginnings, under Mayor Low, of a government for the people. Do the New Yorkers know it? Do they care? They are Americans, mixed and typical; do we Americans really want good government? Or, as I said at starting, have they worked for thirty years along the wrong road—crowded with unhappy American cities—the road to . . . despair?

2 / THE TENEMENT HOUSE PROBLEM

Urged by Governor Theodore Roosevelt, the New York State Legislature authorized the creation of the New York State Tenement Commission of 1900. Robert W. de Forest, president of the New York Charity Organization Society, became its chairman and Lawrence Veiller, secretary of the COS Tenement House Committee, was secretary of the Commission. The Commission and its subsequent Report *and the legislation which resulted from it were largely the work of Veiller, perhaps this country's foremost foe of the tenement. The first item is from the* Report *itself; the second is an example of the testimony heard by the Commission.*

The Typical New York Tenement

Some knowledge of the prevailing kind of New York tenement house must necessarily precede any consideration of its evils and

SOURCE: Robert W. de Forest and Lawrence Veiller, eds., *The Tenement House Problem, including the Report of the New York State Tenement House Commission of 1900* (New York: Macmillan, 1903), pp. 7–9, 389–94.

their remedies. It is known as the "double-decker," "dumb-bell" tenement, a type which New York has the unenviable distinction of having invented. It is a type unknown to any other city in America or Europe.

Although the housing problem is one of the leading political questions of the day in England, the conditions which exist there are ideal compared to the conditions in New York. The tall tenement house, accommodating as many as 100 to 150 persons in one building, extending up six or seven stories into the air, with dark, unventilated rooms, is unknown in London or in any other city of Great Britain. It was first constructed in New York about the year 1879, and with slight modifications has been practically the sole type of building erected since, and is the type of the present day. It is a building usually five or six or even seven stories high, about 25 feet wide, and built upon a lot of land of the same width and about 100 feet deep. The building as a rule extends back 90 feet, leaving the small space of ten feet unoccupied at the rear, so that the back rooms may obtain some light and air. This space has continued to be left open only because the law has compelled it. Upon the entrance floor there are generally two stores, one on each side of the building, and these sometimes have two or three living rooms back of them. In the centre is the entrance hallway, a long corridor less than 3 feet wide and extending back 60 feet in length. This hallway is nearly always totally dark, receiving no light except that from the street door and a faint light that comes from the small windows opening upon the stairs, which are placed at one side of the hallway. Each floor above is generally divided into four sets of apartments, there being seven rooms on each side of the hall, extending back from the street to the rear of the building. The front apartments generally consist of four rooms each and the rear apartments of three rooms, making altogether fourteen upon each floor, or in a seven-story house eighty-four rooms exclusive of the stores and rooms back of them. Of these fourteen rooms on each floor, only four receive direct light and air from the street or from the small yard at the back of the building. Generally, along each side of the building is what is termed an "air shaft," being an indentation of the wall to a depth of about 28 inches, and extending in length for a space of from 50 to 60 feet. This shaft is entirely enclosed on four sides, and is, of course, the full height of the building, often from 60 to 72 feet high. The ostensible purpose of the shaft is to provide light and air to the five rooms on each side of the house which get no direct light and air from the street or yard; but as the shafts are narrow and high, being enclosed on all four sides, and without any intake of air at the bottom, these rooms obtain, instead of fresh air and sunshine, foul air and semi-darkness. Indeed it is questionable whether the rooms would not be more habitable and more sanitary with no shaft at all, depending for their light and air solely upon the front and back rooms into which they open; for each family, besides having the foul air from its own rooms to breathe, is compelled to breathe the emanations from the rooms of some eleven other families; nor is this all, these shafts act as conveyors of noise, odors, and disease, and when fire breaks out serve as inflammable flues, often rendering it impossible to save the buildings from destruction.

A family living in such a building pays for four rooms of this kind a rent of from $12 to $18 a month. Of these four rooms only two are large enough to be deserving of the name of rooms. The front one is generally about 10 feet 6 inches wide by 11 feet 3 inches long; this the family use as a parlor, and often at night, when the small bedrooms opening upon the air shaft are so close and ill-ventilated that sleep is impossible, mattresses are dragged upon the floor of the parlor, and there the family sleep, all together in one room. In summer the small bedrooms are so hot and stifling that a large part of the tenement house population sleep on the roofs, the sidewalks, and the fire-escapes. The other room, the kitchen, is generally the same size as the parlor upon which it opens, and receives all its light and air from the "air shaft," or such a supply as may come to it from the front room. Behind these two rooms are the bedrooms, so called, which are hardly more than closets, being each about 7 feet wide and 8 feet 6 inches long, hardly large enough to contain a bed. These rooms get no light and air whatsoever, except that which comes from the "air shaft," and except on the highest stories are generally almost totally dark. Upon the opposite side of the public hall is an apartment containing four exactly similar rooms, and at the rear of the building there are, instead of four rooms on each side of the hallway, but three, one of the bedrooms being dispensed with. For these three rooms in the rear the rent is generally throughout the city from $10 to $15 a month. In the public hallway, opposite the stairs, there are provided two water-closets, each water-closet being used in common by two families and being lighted and ventilated by the "air shaft," which also lights and ventilates all the bedrooms. In the newer buildings there is frequently provided, in the hallway between the two closets, a dumb-waiter for the use of the tenants.

It is not to be wondered at, therefore, that with such a kind of tenement house repeated all over the different parts of this city, and forming practically the only kind of habitation for the great mass of the people, the tenement house system has become fraught with so much danger to the welfare of the community. The effect upon the city population of the form of congregated living found in our tenement houses is to be seen, not only in its results upon the health of the people, but upon their moral and social condition as well. The public mind is just now especially aroused over the manifestation of one special form of vice in tenement districts. It is not to be wondered at that vice in various forms should manifest itself in the tenements; the wonder is that there is not more vice in such districts. The tenement districts of New York are places in which thousands of people are living in the smallest space in which it is possible for human beings to exist—crowded together in dark, ill-ventilated rooms, in many of which the sunlight never enters and in most of which fresh air is unknown. They are centres of disease, poverty, vice, and crime, where it is a marvel, not that some children grow up to be thieves, drunkards, and prostitutes, but that so many should ever grow up to be decent and self-respecting. All the conditions which surround childhood, youth, and womanhood in New York's crowded tenement quarters make for unrighteousness. They also make for disease. There is hardly a tenement house in which there has not been at least one case of pulmonary tuberculosis within the last five years, and in some houses there have been as great a number as twenty-two different cases of this terrible disease. From the tenements there comes a stream of sick, helpless people to our hospitals and dispensaries, few of whom are able to afford the luxury of a private physician, and some houses are in such bad sanitary condition that few people can be seriously ill in them and get well; from them also comes a host of paupers and charity seekers. The most terrible of all the features of tenement house life in New York, however, is the indiscriminate herding of all kinds of people in close contact, the fact, that, mingled with the drunken, the dissolute, the improvident, the diseased, dwell the great mass of the respectable working-men of the city with their families. . . .

. . . . .

MY EXPERIENCE OF LIFE IN A SECOND-CLASS TENEMENT-FLAT HOUSE

[The writer of the following is the wife of a stationary engineer occupying a position which enables them now to live in better quarters than the average tenement house provides. During the time of which she writes her husband was a fireman with irregular work, and they lived in a tenement house, paying $11 per month for three rooms.]

Why I say second-class is there are three classes, first, second, and third. First-class, in which you pay high rent for location and appearance of house and hallways. Generally the rooms are small, but you have bath-room, range, and improvements.

Second-class, in which you pay reasonable rent and get good-sized rooms, but no improvements and poor location. It is this class I have seen the most of, because I have lived in them, and, of course, they are the homes of the respectable (or supposed to be) working class; although the classes of people get all mixed together according to circumstances. If you put on your thinking cap, you need not lack work for the brain, and if you are observing you need not lack amusement. But you must have no nerves, or you live a life of excitement and nervousness. Before I was married I had never lived in a tenement flat. My first experience I felt like a prisoner. I knew I was free, but I felt as if some power was keeping me there against my will.

After I got used to the life, I began to look around and study things up, and to wonder why I should feel like that. I began to study my neighbors, and I found if you want to live in peace, you must keep to yourself. I saw some gossiping and drinking together to-day, and to-morrow fighting; and not content with fighting among themselves, they draw their husbands into it, when they come home from work. Then there are some who want to borrow all the time from every one. Then you see men, and women too, going for drink as early as five o'clock A.M. The women will neglect their homes, children, husbands, and everything for drink; they never seem sober.

That is where the danger of fire comes, with such people; for they are not responsible for their actions, or able to control their children. I have seen children playing, running to and fro with blazing paper. One night we were preparing for rest when there was a smell of fire. I opened the room door and saw the hallways full of smoke and all the people out on the stairs. Two or three of us ran down to the janitor, and we saw black smoke coming from the front rooms on the ground floor. We knocked and knocked till at last an old woman opened the door. She was just rags and dirt, and too drunk to speak. The washtubs were full of clothes, colored and white, all mixed together; she said she was washing. There was no fire, but a small lamp stood on the stove burning; coal was scattered all over the floor; the place was upside down, and whiskey bottles were all over the window-sill. The place had such a close smell, no bed made, and it past 10 P.M. The place was a picture of filth and dirt, and yet the furniture and other things were good. She said there was nothing burning there, and we could not find where the smoke came from, although the room kept filling with black smoke. We searched the cellar, but no smoke was there. So we had to retire at that. Lovely sensation to go to rest with not knowing what hour you may be awakened by fire!

Another time it was Sunday noontime; we had just sat down to dinner when I saw smoke up the air shaft. I thought at first it was fog, then it grew blacker, and I ran into the hallway, and looking over the banister I saw the smoke thick and I heard voices; so I called out, "What is the matter down there?" and a voice said in a scared whisper, "The house is on fire." I ran into the room, and slipping on my best shoes I snatched up my clothes that I had laid on the bed ready to go out after dinner. I took a towel and wound it round my head and face, telling my husband to do the same quickly. I groped my way downstairs and out into the street just as the flames were bursting through under the stairs. I ran up the street a few houses to where the agent's office was, and left my things, thinking my husband was following me with his things, but no. Then I ran back to find him; he was looking for me, and had nothing. He said I was so quick that he did not know what was happening, and when he saw the flames he came down to see if I was out safe; then he wanted to go back, but the firemen would not let him, for the house was cleared of every one. The smoke was dense.

Well, after it was all over we went back. We lived on the third floor, and the fire had just begun to come through under the wash-tubs and in the bedroom. All the lower stairs and ground floor and first floor back was destroyed. It appears that two weeks before they had let the back basement to a man and his wife with two children; they had very little furniture, and four days before the fire they had the furniture insured, and on Sunday had filled the ash cans full of rags and set fire to it. The fire marshal had the man arrested. Had it been night no one would have escaped. That is one reason why landlords should have tenements fireproof.

Another delightful thing is the smell of cooking; you get sniffs of all kinds, sometimes not very fresh, so that by the time you are ready for your own dinner you have no appetite.

Nice quiet life in a tenement! On one floor you will find two families living next door to each other, very neighborly for a time, going from room to room; then they drink together day after day, night after night, until husbands and wives get all mixed up; then they all fight, tearing and biting each other like animals, and getting knives to each other. Of course at a time like that all the men, women, and children that are in the house are out on the stairs and in the hallways.

Over us lived a man and wife with two children; they were so ragged and filthy I was glad when they moved. Then came a young couple; really they looked boy and girl—he looked about twenty-one and she about eighteen; they were supposed to be married three months only. Another young man used to visit them. For two days and nights they danced, they shouted. I cannot call it singing, because they were too drunk to sing. Well, it was like bedlam let loose. We could not sleep, for they kept it up early and late. We did not like to say anything, or make a complaint, for we thought they were having their honeymoon. It was summer time, and every window was open, so everything could be heard. He would become quarrelsome, and they would both swear like troopers. They were not so innocent as they looked. They kept it up two or three times a week for three months. The people began to shout at them from different houses, to keep quiet and let people sleep. The answer they got was, "I am an American citizen." At last people complained to the agent. Then they began to throw furniture about and hammer on the doors. So the agent asked me if they were as bad as people said, for he said I must have the worst of it, as I lived under them. I showed him the ceiling, all broken and cracked all over, so that I expected it to come down. So they had to move. Then another family came, with two children, a boy of about eight years, and a girl of about six years. Both father and mother drank; he beat his wife, and she beat the children; they were bruised and cut all over. I heard the boy screaming, "Oh, mamma, please don't hit me." With that, it sounded as if she had taken the poker or something from the stove. She must have hit him, for he screamed more, and said, "Oh, mamma, mamma, my head is bleeding." I was going to report them to the Gerry society.

Then you can watch your neighbors in other houses, and put two and two together and tell what is happening. I saw husband and wife so comfortable and happy together every morning and evening. One morning I saw the man go out early, and about ten o'clock I heard crying and moaning. I listened, and thought, that is not a child; that is a woman in distress. I looked and saw people in the room. I thought, something has happened. So later on in the day I heard he was killed by the train. After the funeral she moved away. Some one moving in and out nearly every day.

The back of the house in the next street was empty except two floors. On one floor were two old ladies, so prim and severe looking they reminded me of New England women. On the other floor was man and wife. I think the man was a musician that played at parties or in the street; for twice a week two men would come and practise with him. One played bass fiddle, and the other a harp, while he played the violin. After they had practised a time they would play dance music, and all the girls and boys in the flats would go in the yards and dance. How the people did enjoy that music! Every one would be at their windows listening. Sometimes they would play old song tunes, so soft, and so beautiful. Then the people would clap their hands; it was inspiring in a neighborhood like that. I was sorry when they left.

At last the top floor was let to a family with two children. One little tot about three years old would climb up and hang through the window; I expected him to fall every day. When the next floor was let to a young couple, with a baby a few weeks old, they were friends of the people over them; so they all had a jollification together in the upper rooms, drinking, music, and dancing about till late. The next night the young man was putting down the carpet and beside him was the beer can; they were drinking beer all evening. About a week after they gave, what I suppose they call, a housewarming, and there were lively times till early morning. About a week after that, on Thursday night, I heard the baby crying day and night. I thought, that baby is sick; the third night I did not hear it, so I thought it was better. On Sunday my husband said to me, they are having another party over the way; they have company and they are all dressed up. I looked and saw white flowers on the fire-escape. I said, "Why, it is a funeral party; the baby is dead." So they moved away. (Another picture in the panorama of life!)

It is a mystery to me whether drink causes poverty or poverty causes drink among the working classes. Of course, there are many things the landlord cannot help. If he turns out bad tenants, he is likely to get worse, or as bad. If he wishes to keep his house quiet and respectable, he must get references with his tenants. The landlords cannot always help the overcrowding, for when a person goes after rooms, they are asked how many in family; oh, three; but when they move in there are uncles and aunts, and perhaps boarders, making double the number. Sometimes one family will rent the rooms, and two families move in.

There is much the landlords can do for the good of their tenants. For instance, it is the landlord's duty, or agent's, to see that the janitor keeps the place clean. It is dreadful to see the condition of the air shafts: they are cleaned when it suits the janitors; they are the receptacle for everything thrown from the windows of two houses; a child naturally throws things through the windows, but grown people should know better,—they are as bad as the children. Bones, skins of fruit, old tin cans, dirty paper, and all kinds of things are thrown out. It ought to be the duty of the Board of Health to see that the landlords attend to these things. I do not think the Board of Health inspectors should say when they are going around; they should take the people by surprise and they would see many things.

Then, again, spitting on stairs and in hallways should be strictly forbidden, and not only forbidden, but made punishable by law. There should be a light kept in the dark lower hallway at all times, for the hall and stairs are so narrow, a person coming down and a person going up are likely to collide, especially if they are carrying anything. Anything that is detrimental to the health of others should not be allowed. If people would only think of the golden rule, to do to others as they wish to be done by, and think that the world was not made for them alone. For those that are compelled to live in tenements, how they could help each other to live better and happier lives. Some one may be sick or dying, and they are disturbed. Those that are trying to better the conditions of the poor have much to study and many problems to solve, that will take time and patience. It may seem disheartening to an onlooker, for he cannot see the ins and outs like a person that lives among the poor.

There is one thing especially I think is dreadful, and I think it is the cause of a great many children being so rude and forward. In the ordinary flats there is no privacy at all, either from your children or your neighbors; for everything can be heard unless you are as quiet as a deaf and dumb person. Of course people do not always whisper. Now there are many little things about private business that husband and wife wish to talk about, that concern no one else. If in building the new model houses they would make the walls and floors to deaden sound, it would be a great blessing to humanity. The Association for Improving the Condition of the Poor has done much toward baths for the people; but it would be a great benefit to many a poor family if they would build baths for washing and drying clothes, charging so much an hour, as they have in London, for in small flats where there are children, washing is very unhealthy, drying clothes where people eat and sleep, when the weather is bad. If you hang them on the roof you must watch them or they disappear; if you live in the back and have pulley lines, in some places a sheet and one tablecloth fills the line, and they blow over the next line, and get more dirty than before they were washed. The women up over you shake their bedclothes and rugs over your clothes; and if the people are not clean, then your clothes will have animals walking about over them.

Oh, there is lots to think about in a tenement-flat house. Talk about fire-escapes, for so they are called! I should call them curiosity shops, for they are covered with everything from bedding down to flower-pots; here you see rags of quilts and clothes; there you see chairs, tin boxes, ice boxes, dogs, birds, cats, rabbits, jars, and bottles of every description, big parrots screeching at each other, canaries singing, and children playing. Here and there you will find a fire-escape devoted to flowers alone, but rarely. They are a sight to see. When I look through my windows and down between the rows of houses, where the yards are so small that the houses seem quite close together, it reminds me of the old historical Petticoat Lane, Whitechapel, in London.

I leave the third class entirely out, for it is past my comprehension how they live at all. It is only an animal existence—work, eat, sleep, drink. No thought of cleanliness in homes or themselves. That class is the hardest to reach. It is a problem how to deal with them, to better their condition. It is of no use whatever talking or preaching to them. The only way I see is force of example through their children. When they see the children growing up to be what they should be, they will be ashamed if they are not too hardened and stupid with drink. If they do not entirely reform, they will keep within bounds for their children's sakes, and the children will be able to do a great deal with their parents.

3 / CAPITALISM THE CAUSE, SOCIALISM THE CURE

In 1902, the veteran labor leader and five-time Socialist candidate for President, Eugene V. Debs, provided this unsolicited reply to the query of a Chicago journalist.

For some days William E. Curtis, the far-famed correspondent of the Chicago *Record-Herald,* has been pressing the above inquiry upon representative people of all classes with a view to throwing all possible light upon that vexed subject.

SOURCE: Eugene V. Debs, "What's the Matter with Chicago?" *Writings and Speeches of Eugene V. Debs* (New York: Hermitage Press, 1948), pp. 50–54.

The inquiry is in such general terms and takes such wide scope that anything like a comprehensive answer would fill a book without exhausting the subject, while a review of the "interviews" would embrace the whole gamut of absurdity and folly and produce a library of comedy and tragedy.

Not one of the replies I have seen has sufficient merit to be printed in a paper read by grown folks, and those that purport to come from leaders of labor and representatives of the working class take the prize in what would appear to be a competitive contest for progressive asininity.

The leader, so-called, who puts it upon record in a capitalist paper and gives the libel the widest circulation, that Chicago is alright, so far as the workers are concerned, that they have plenty and are prosperous and happy, is as fit to lead the working class as is a wolf to guide a flock of spring lambs.

It is from the wage worker's point of view that I shall attempt an answer to the question propounded by Mr. Curtis, and in dealing with the subject I shall be as candid as may be expected from a Socialist agitator.

The question is opportune at this season, when the "frost is on the pumpkin," and the ballot is soon to decide to what extent the people really know "What is the matter with Chicago."

First of all, Chicago is the product of modern capitalism, and, like all other great commercial centers, is unfit for human habitation. The Illinois Central Railroad Company selected the site upon which the city is built and this consisted of a vast miasmatic swamp far better suited to mosquito culture than for human beings. From the day the site was chosen by (and of course in the interest of all) said railway company, everything that entered into the building of the town and the development of the city was determined purely from profit considerations and without the remotest concern for the health and comfort of the human beings who were to live there, especially those who had to do all the labor and produce all the wealth.

As a rule hogs are only raised where they have good health and grow fat. Any old place will do to raise human beings.

At this very hour typhoid fever and diphtheria are epidemic

in Chicago and the doctors agree that these ravages are due to the microbes and germs generated in the catchbasins and sewers which fester and exhale their foul and fetid breath upon the vast swarms of human beings caught and fettered there.

Thousands upon thousands of Chicago's population have been poisoned to death by the impure water and foul atmosphere of this undrainable swamp (notwithstanding the doctored mortuary tables by which it is proven to prospective investors that it is the healthiest city on earth) and thousands more will commit suicide in the same way, but to compensate for it all Chicago has the prize location for money-making, immense advantage for profit-mongering—and what are human beings compared to money?

During recent years Chicago has expended millions to lift herself out of her native swamp, but the sewage floats back to report the dismal failure of the attempt, and every germ-laden breeze confirms the report.

That is one thing that is the matter with Chicago. It never was intended that human beings should live there. A thousand sites infinitely preferable for a city could have been found in close proximity, but they lacked the "commercial" advantages which are of such commanding importance in the capitalist system.

And now they wonder "What is the matter with Chicago!" Look at some of her filthy streets in the heart of the city, chronically torn up, the sunlight obscured, the air polluted, the water contaminated, every fountain and stream designed to bless the race poisoned at its source—and you need not wonder what ails Chicago, nor will you escape the conclusion that the case is chronic and that the present city will never recover from the fatal malady.

What is true of Chicago physically is emphasized in her social, moral and spiritual aspects, and this applies to every commercial metropolis in the civilized world.

From any rational point of view they are all dismal failures.

There is no reason under the sun, aside from the profit considerations of the capitalist system, why two million humans should be stacked up in layers and heaps until they jar the clouds, while millions of acres of virgin soil are totally uninhabited.

The very contemplation of the spectacle gives rise to serious doubt as to the sanity of the race.

Such a vast population in such a limited area cannot feed itself, has not room to move and cannot keep clean.

The deadly virus of capitalism is surging through all the veins of this young mistress of trade and the eruptions are found all over the body social and politic, and that's "What's the matter with Chicago."

Hundreds of the *Record-Herald's* quacks are prescribing their nostrums for the blotches and pustules which have broken out upon the surface, but few have sense enough to know and candor enough to admit that the virus must be expelled from the system —and these few are Socialists who are so notoriously visionary and impracticable that their opinions are not worthy of space in a great paper printed to conserve the truth and promote the welfare of society.

This model metropolis of the West has broken all the records for political corruption. Her old rival on the Mississippi, catching the inspiration doubtless, has been making some effort to crown herself with similar laurels, but for smooth political jobbery and fancy manipulation of the wires, Chicago is still far in the lead. In the "Windy City" ward politics has long been recognized as a fine art and the collection is unrivalled anywhere.

From the millions of dollars filched from the millions of humans by the corporate owners of the common utilities, the reeking corruption funds flow like lava tides, and to attempt to purify the turbid stream by the "reform measures" proposed from time to time by the Republican-Democratic Party in its internal conflict for the spoils of office, is as utter a piece of folly as to try with beeswax to seal up Mount Pelée.

Chicago has plutocrats and paupers in the ratio of more than sixteen to one—boulevards for the exhibition of the rich and alleys for the convenience of the poor.

Chicago has also a grand army of the most skilled pickpockets, artistic confidence operators, accomplished foot-pads and adept cracksmen on earth. So well is this understood that on every breeze we hear the refrain:

> "When Reuben comes to town,
> He's sure to be done brown—"

And this lugubrious truth is treated as the richest of jokes, with utter unconsciousness of the moral degeneracy it reflects, the crime it glorifies and the indictment of capitalist society it returns in answer to the *Record-Herald's* query: "What's the matter with Chicago"?

Besides the array of "talent" above mentioned, fostered by competitive society everywhere, the marshy metropolis by the lake may boast of a vast and flourishing gambling industry, an illimitable and progressive "levee" district, sweatshops, slums, dives, bloated men, bedraggled women, ghastly caricatures of their former selves, babies cradled in rags and filth, aged children, than which nothing could be more melancholy—all these and a thousand more, the fruit of our present social anarchy, afflict Chicago; and worst of all, our wise social philosophers, schooled in the economics of capitalist universities, preach the comforting doctrine that all these are necessary evils and at best can but be restricted within certain bounds; and this hideous libel is made a cloak that theft may continue to masquerade as philanthropy.

It is at this point that Chicago particularly prides herself upon her "charities," hospitals and eleemosynary endowments, all breathing the sweet spirit of Christian philanthropy—utterly ignorant of the fact, designedly or otherwise, that these very institutions are manifestations of social disease and are monumental of the iniquity of the system that must rear such whited sepulchres to conceal its crimes.

I do not oppose the insane asylum—but I abhor and condemn the cut-throat system that robs man of his reason, drives him to insanity and makes the lunatic asylum an indispensable adjunct to every civilized community.

With the ten thousand "charities" that are proposed to poultice the sores and bruises of society, I have little patience.

Worst of all is the charity ball. Chicago indulges in these festering festivals on a grand scale.

Think of cavorting around in a dress suit because some poor wretch is hungry; and of indulging in a royal carousal to comfort some despairing woman on the brink of suicide; and finally, that in "fashionable society" the definition of this mixture of inanity and moral perversion is "charity."

Fleece your fellows! That is "business," and you are a captain of industry. Having "relieved" your victims of their pelts, dance and make merry to "relieve" their agony. This is "charity" and you are a philanthropist.

In summing up the moral assets of a great (?) city, the churches should not be overlooked. Chicago is a city of fine churches. All the denominations are copiously represented, and sermons in all languages and of all varieties are turned out in job lots and at retail to suit the market.

The churches are always numerous where vice is rampant. They seem to spring from the same soil and thrive in the same climate.

And yet the churches are supposed to wage relentless warfare upon evil. To just what extent they have checked its spread in the "Windy City" may be inferred from the probing of the press into the body social to ascertain "What is the matter with Chicago."

The preachers are not wholly to blame, after all, for their moral and spiritual impotency. They are wage-workers, the same as coal miners, and are just as dependent upon the capitalist class. How can they be expected to antagonize the interests of their employers and hold their jobs? The unskilled preachers, the common laborers in the arid spots of the vineyard, are often wretchedly paid, and yet they remain unorganized and have never struck for better wages.

"What's the matter with Chicago"? Capitalism!

What's the cure? Socialism!

Regeneration will only come with depopulation—when Socialism has relieved the congestion and released the people and they spread out over the country and live close to the grass.

The *Record-Herald* has furnished the people of Chicago and Illinois with a campaign issue.

If you want to know more about "What is the matter with Chicago," read the Socialist papers and magazines; read the platform of the Socialist Party; and if you do, you will cut loose from the Republican-Democratic Party, the double-headed political monstrosity of the capitalist class, and you will cast your vote for the Socialist Party and your lot with the International Socialist Movement, whose mission it is to uproot and overthrow the whole system of capitalist exploitation, and put an end to the poverty and misery it entails—and that's "What's the matter with Chicago."

4 / BEAUTIFICATION

The City Beautiful movement, inspired by the Columbian Exposition of 1894, aimed at keeping its momentum rolling at the St. Louis Fair scheduled for 1903. William S. Crandall, editor of the Municipal Journal and Engineer, *suggests that a model city at the Fair might encourage urban dwellers to beautify their cities.*

The American tourist, when rambling through the old cities of Europe whose history antedates, perhaps, the discovery of the Western Hemisphere, constantly remarks upon the seeming lack of plan or purpose. The cities apparently grew haphazard, and streets were laid out without reference to artistic effect and without proper regard for transportation facilities. Indeed, what-

SOURCE: William S. Crandall, "The Model City: A Suggestion for the St. Louis Exposition," *Municipal Affairs,* V (September, 1901), 670–74.

ever of plan there is to be found in European cities, has its origin, in most instances, in the last century, and very frequently within the last quarter of it. Paris—the Mecca of students of civic æsthetics—is the product of Baron Haussmann and his immediate successors, many of whom are still active. The broad avenues, the commodious public buildings, the spacious parks of Berlin, London, Vienna, Glasgow and hundreds of other cities are the work of yesterday. A description of sanitary conditions in almost every city of fifty years ago is so strange and appalling as to cause its accuracy to be challenged. A well-constructed sewage system, which we have come to assume as properly belonging to every progressive city, is wholly the outgrowth of the last generation of sanitary engineers. It is only a short time ago that street cleaning departments began their existence, and such scavenging as was done was performed by the dog, the hog or the buzzard.

There is now, however, a well-developed science for all the various lines of municipal activity; and however far short of perfection actual administration may fall, not even the most pessimistic person will contend that rapid progress has not been made. The narrative of such progress ought to be an inspiration to every public official and to every urban dweller.

The principal defect at the present moment is the lack of facilities for placing the experience of widely-separated cities at the disposal of each and every urban center. Every city has its own peculiar local conditions, out of which spring peculiar problems that sometimes require treatment considerably different from that adopted by other cities. Nevertheless, what has been tried and has succeeded or has failed, is of great value to every other city, for thereby much experimentation, much time and much expense may be saved.

Then, too, there is competition between cities, as well as between individuals. Persons of wealth, and, to some extent, the central offices of business houses, locate where municipal improvements have been carried farthest. The city that has poorly-paved streets, hideous public buildings, inadequate sewage systems, and poor water supplies cannot long compete with its more progressive and better-governed neighbor. Good Americans are said to go to Paris when they die, not because Paris is considered the commercial center of the world, but because it is considered the most beautiful city. Art, therefore, is a very important factor, and every city which wishes to retain its position and grow in wealth and population, must know what other cities are doing, and learn from their experience.

It was the appreciation of these facts—the inspiration that would come from a comparison of past and present conditions, and the benefits of a more general familiarity with the best each city affords—that led the Municipal Art Society of New York to suggest to the authorities of the Louisiana Purchase Exposition the construction of a model city and a municipal art exhibit at St. Louis in 1903.

The memorial presented suggested:

First—That those departments of the general Exposition which are similar in their functions to the same departments in modern cities be incorporated as working models in the general plan of the special Exposition. These may include the engineering, park and tree planting, fire, police, health, street cleaning, garbage disposal, water supply, and other departments. These may be so grouped as to illustrate the administration of a modern city on the best lines and thus form an object lesson for American and foreign cities without the least interference with their normal functions as necessities of the Exposition itself.

Second—There are certain other features, which, while not in themselves necessities to the welfare of the Exposition, would be valuable educational attractions. Public schools, public library, museum and similar buildings devoted to educational matters would naturally be included.

Third—Any plans for a model city would involve treatment of parks and plaza spaces, street crossing and other vistas, grouping and architecture of other structures and other lines in which the aesthetic factor is important. To make these practical, however, they must be adjusted to more utilitarian features (as in the case of actual practice); hence are thus suggested rather than definitely specified.

Fourth—In order that there might be a place for the assemblage and classification of the smaller concrete objects, such as street signs, lamp posts, letter boxes, paper receptacles, park settees, street electroliers, street cleaning machinery, and a thousand and one other articles employed in the construction and maintenance of a city, a building to be called the Municipal Art Building might be erected.

The proposed scheme is so broad in its scope and so comprehensive in its opportunity as to render difficult a concise statement. Its general purpose is to show (1) the progress already made in every phase of municipal development, (2) the most successful methods of solving each and every municipal problem, beginning with the laying out of a city (streets, avenues, parks, etc.) and ending with the public baths, laundries, theatres and telephones, having run the entire gamut of municipal problems and city conditions, and (3) how art may be combined with utility so as to make the city not only the most effective industrial, commercial and social unit, but also the most attractive and the most beautiful.

To this end plans, photographs and sketches should be secured from the most progressive cities of the world, and, wherever possible, the machinery actually used should be displayed. For instance, Chicago should send a working model of the sanitary canal by which it disposes of its sewage. Paris should exhibit its system of sewers. Glasgow might be called upon to portray its well-developed system of garbage disposal and utilization. New York would explain the rapid transit subway it is now building —the most extensive system in the world.

Private companies would gladly display the various kinds of machinery and manufactured products used by cities or private corporations doing municipal work, such as fire apparatus, garbage incinerators, paving materials, water meters, filters, hydrants, etc., sewer appliances, lighting systems, voting machines, etc., etc. Wherever possible this display would be supplemented by practical illustration. Fire companies from various cities could give drills showing latest and most approved methods of fighting fires and saving life. The streets of the Exposition would be cleaned in the best possible way, and garbage disposal works erected upon the grounds.

In other instances, where it is impossible, owing to lack of space or of facilities for doing the work, stereopticon views and moving pictures could be used very effectively, and the visitor to the Exposition thus enabled to see what the cities of the world were doing for their citizens, without visiting them personally.

Particular attention should be paid to public art, and the cities of the world sacked to secure the most artistic lamp posts, street signs, guideboards, public buildings, bridges, monuments, parks, boulevards, railway stations, etc., etc. Heretofore, principal attention has been paid to utility, but the fact is now becoming widely recognized that art and utility can easily be combined, and that the public appreciates, yea, even demands, the most artistic, rather than the hideous or even the commonplace.

Such an exhibit of models, photographs, sketches and drawings from the world's cities would be one of the most attractive features of the Exposition, in connection with which there could be held an International Convention upon Public Art. Two have already been held in Paris and Brussels; the third is soon to be held at Turin.

The advantages of such an exhibit are so evident as to call for little discussion. The Model City would be an inspiration to every city dweller and public official. It would show in a way which no one could escape, the possibility as well as the advisability of solving every problem in the most effective manner.

The increasing concentration of population warns us that every social and political problem is to be settled, if settled at all, in the cities, and with city conditions plainly in mind. From one-third to two-thirds of the inhabitants of every progressive country reside in cities over ten thousand population, and the censuses just being taken indicate that we have hardly crossed the threshold.

Yet, up to the present time, there has been no specific effort made to interest the city visitor. No exposition, little or big, ignores the agricultural population. It is safe to say that a large majority of the visitors of any exposition comes from the incorporated municipalities. Assuming this to be a correct statement, is it not about time that the city, town and village be recognized in some manner befitting their importance? An effort is made to teach the farmer; why not make an equal effort for the benefit of the citizen who has to provide his own government? . . .

. . . . .

Chicago gave to the world "The White City" in 1893, Buffalo its "Rainbow City" in 1901, and now let St. Louis contribute "The Model City."

5 / THE SETTLEMENT AND THE INSTITUTIONAL CHURCH

In 1907, the Reverend Josiah Strong, a leading spokesman for the Social Gospel, circularized a large number of settlements and institutional churches, requesting them to comment on the usefulness of their work. Three of the replies are typical of the entire group.

CHURCH OF THE HOLY COMMUNION, NEW YORK (REV. HENRY MOTTET, D.D., PASTOR)

In answer to your circular communication, which makes a particularly strong appeal to me, I beg to answer as follows, asking you to bear in mind that I have been closely identified with the work of this parish for practically forty years:

1. I can educe definite and even minute evidence of the fact that vice, crime, and pauperism have largely decreased in this neighborhood during that time.

2. That judging from the history of our work among the young, which has always been one of the strong characteristics of this parish, juvenile delinquency has been almost eliminated.

3. That the sanitary conditions under which the people of this

SOURCE: Josiah Strong, *The Challenge of the City* (New York: Young People's Missionary Movement, 1907), pp. 286–87, 294–98.

vicinage now live are a paradise compared to what they were forty years ago.

4. The very marked and strong disposition of foreigners coming into our midst is to obtain the advantage as quickly as possible given to them by American citizenship.

5. This church has taken hold vigorously in the purification of politics, in the work of the primaries, and in the development of the independent voter. I confess I feel very proud of the results we have achieved. Less than two years ago a notorious ward politician acknowledged to me that the influence of this church was making it more difficult to buy votes.

6. With the aid of our police captain we watch the saloons and other establishments of doubtful morality, and we lose no opportunity in having them closed. One man wishing to open a saloon came and confessed that if I would consent he might obtain a license, and he was foolish enough to offer me one thousand dollars for my consent. Having asked him to put his proposition in writing over his signature he withdrew. He was never heard from again and he never obtained the license.

I think that our police captain, as well as the people of the neighborhood who have large business interests, will bear me out in the statement that forty years have wrought a very remarkable change for the better in this section of the city.

I recall the time when some of the vilest dens of vice and some of the most dangerous haunts of criminals were actually within the sound of this church bell.

South End House, Boston (Robert A. Woods, Head of the House)

The police recognize, very cordially, the value of our work in reducing the amount of disorder in the neighborhood.

This Settlement has had a leading share, both in the establishment and in the administration of the Dover Street Bath House and the Ward 9 Gymnasium. It was active in securing for the district the South End Playground and, in its present admirable form, the South End Branch of the Public Library; and it has been making successful efforts toward broadening the usefulness of both. It has also had a considerable part in the whole movement which has led up to the establishment of the Franklin Union, now in process of erection on the borders of the South End House neighborhood. When this great evening technical institute is complete, and taking into account the Evening High School, also located near by, these six progressive municipal institutions will, it is believed, constitute the most remarkable combination in the way of municipal effort for social improvement to be found in any similar city district in the world.

A clear result of all this work is found in the better physical type represented by the young men and young women of the neighborhood as compared with those who were at the same stage in life ten years ago. While statistics for the neighborhood by itself are not available, it is beyond question that it holds its own with other neighborhoods throughout the city in the proved decrease in juvenile law-breaking. There has been a noticeable improvement in the matter of peace and order, and even in the freedom from bad language. The low-grade characters, which were a large company, are dead; and many of their places are not filled. The young men who are coming on have had warnings on the one hand and incitements on the other; a social sense fixed on somewhat better things is alive in them.

In the homes of the neighborhood there is a noticeably better standard as to sanitation, cooking, and the welfare of the children. There is somewhat more intelligent expenditure on food, on clothing and furniture. The habit of thrift has grown, under persistent practical encouragement. Not a few families, becoming involved in the hospitalities of the neighborhood, have moved out of three-room into four-room tenements in order that they might have a parlor. Many new and uplifting interests have arisen which have kindled a more lively and more generous sort of family and neighborhood intercourse.

The Boys' Club has, to a great extent, done away with the boys' gang. The lesson and example of fair and effective association has not been without effect upon independent local clubs of young men. A measure of neighborhood loyalty, cropping out in connection with the success of a dramatic club or an athletic team, or at one of the neighborhood reunions, has come unmistakably into being. The organization of the scattered local forces of good-will is on the way; and this means the moral recuperation of the neighborhood.

The House has been able to render certain distinctive contributions toward municipal reform in Boston. In the first place, it has made plain by its studies the actual underlying nature of local machine politics. Secondly, it has pointed out clearly that local political corruption depends largely upon the leverage which it gains upon the city treasury through the power of the aldermen. In the third place, it took the lead in securing the passage of a bill by which the aldermen are elected at large, a system which has made it possible to concentrate the vote of good citizens throughout the whole city upon certain aldermanic candidates, with distinctly successful results.

In many detailed ways the workers of the Settlement find their overtures met by a growing spirit of sympathetic understanding and practical coöperation on the part of the teachers in the local schools, representatives of the Board of Health, the police, the authorities of the City Hospital, and many other public officials. Particular attention has been paid to coöperation with the Juvenile Court.

The Forward Movement, Chicago, Illinois (Mary E. Dix, Head Resident)

The social centers of vice with which we have to contend and which are under the patronage of the police power to a greater or less extent are the saloons, the houses of assignation, gambling resorts, and, in some districts, there should be added the midnight school for teaching boys to steal. Over against these are the Settlement influences.

As to the "decrease in vice, crime, and pauperism," I am compelled to say that I think there is not much decrease in the first two; but in the last there has been a very great improvement. Our Settlement has given constant emphasis in favor of self-help and the effect of it is very manifest throughout the neighborhood. The societies that exist professionally for charity are, perhaps, one of the difficulties with which we have to contend.

As to the "decrease in juvenile delinquencies," we have no statistics that we can quote as to the influence of the Settlement directly upon this point. There is a great improvement in the neighborhood, part of which I think should be credited to the Juvenile Court and part to the Settlement.

As to the "improvement in sanitary conditions," I am happy to report that this is very marked, indeed, and I think it is very largely due to the Settlement work, possibly indirectly in the decrease in pauperism or the giving to the people the ability to demand better conditions, else they would vacate such houses as were notoriously bad.

As to the "Americanizing of immigrants," I think the Settlement influence has had much to do through contact with club life, entertainments, libraries, and the instilling of the American spirit: all of which are greatly helped by the public schools of the community.

As to the "increase of civic patriotism," I do not know as we have any basis upon which to form a well-grounded conclusion. There is undoubtedly an increase, because of the things that have preceded this. Our Settlement is located in a largely American district.

As to the "decrease in the number of saloons, policy-shops, dance halls, variety shows," and the like, I am persuaded that the strong arm of the law is about the only thing that affects our district.

6 / THE GHETTO THEATER

When Hutchins Hapgood, a well-to-do American of old stock, prepared these studies of New York's Lower East Side, he was struck by the vitality of the Jewish immigrant quarter in the midst of its unbelievable poverty and squalor. The ability to create and enjoy the most popular theater in the country undoubtedly helped the residents of the ghetto to survive their environment and, ultimately, to leave it.

In the three Yiddish theatres on the Bowery is expressed the world of the Ghetto—that New York City of Russian Jews, large, complex, with a full life and civilization. In the midst of the frivolous Bowery, devoted to tinsel variety shows, "dive" music-halls, fake museums, trivial amusement booths of all sorts, cheap lodging-houses, ten-cent shops and Irish-American tough saloons, the theatres of the chosen people alone present the serious as well as the trivial interests of an entire community. Into these three buildings crowd the Jews of all the Ghetto classes—the sweat-shop woman with her baby, the day-laborer, the small Hester Street shopkeeper, the Russian-Jewish anarchist and socialist, the Ghetto rabbi and scholar, the poet, the journalist. The poor and ignorant are in the great majority, but the learned, the intellectual and the progressive are also represented, and here, as elsewhere, exert a more than numerically proportionate influence on the character of the theatrical productions, which, nevertheless, remain essentially popular. The socialists and the literati create the demand that forces into the mass of vaudeville,

SOURCE: Hutchins Hapgood, *The Spirit of the Ghetto: Studies of the Jewish Quarter of New York* (New York: Funk & Wagnalls Company, 1902), pp. 113–23, 140–41.

light opera, historical and melodramatic plays a more serious art element, a simple transcript from life or the theatric presentation of a Ghetto problem. But this more serious element is so saturated with the simple manners, humor and pathos of the life of the poor Jew, that it is seldom above the heartfelt understanding of the crowd.

The audiences vary in character from night to night rather more than in an up-town theatre. On the evenings of the first four week-days the theatre is let to a guild or club, many hundred of which exist among the working people of the east side. Many are labor organizations representing the different trades, many are purely social, and others are in the nature of secret societies. Some of these clubs are formed on the basis of a common home in Russia. The people, for instance, who came from Vilna, a city in the old country, have organized a Vilna Club in the Ghetto. Then, too, the anarchists have a society; there are many socialistic orders; the newspapers of the Ghetto have their constituency, which sometimes hires the theatre. Two or three hundred dollars is paid to the theatre by the guild, which then sells the tickets among the faithful for a good price. Every member of the society is forced to buy, whether he wants to see the play or not, and the money made over and above the expenses of hiring the theatre is for the benefit of the guild. These performances are therefore called "benefits." The widespread existence of such a custom is a striking indication of the growing sense of corporate interests among the laboring classes of the Jewish east side. It is an expression of the socialistic spirit which is marked everywhere in the Ghetto.

On Friday, Saturday and Sunday nights the theatre is not let, for these are the Jewish holidays, and the house is always completely sold out, altho prices range from twenty-five cents to a dollar. Friday night is, properly speaking, the gala occasion of the week. That is the legitimate Jewish holiday, the night before the Sabbath. Orthodox Jews, as well as others, may then amuse themselves. Saturday, altho the day of worship, is also of holiday character in the Ghetto. This is due to the Christian influences, to which the Jews are more and more sensitive. Through economic necessity Jewish workingmen are compelled to work on Saturday, and, like other workingmen, look upon Saturday night as a holiday, in spite of the frown of the orthodox. Into Sunday, too, they extend their freedom, and so in the Ghetto there are now three popularly recognized nights on which to go with all the world to the theatre.

On those nights the theatre presents a peculiarly picturesque sight. Poor workingmen and women with their babies of all ages fill the theatre. Great enthusiasm is manifested, sincere laughter and tears accompany the sincere acting on the stage. Pedlars of soda-water, candy, of fantastic gewgaws of many kinds, mix freely with the audience between the acts. Conversation during the play is received with strenuous hisses, but the falling of the curtain is the signal for groups of friends to get together and gossip about the play or the affairs of the week. Introductions are not necessary, and the Yiddish community can then be seen and approached with great freedom. On the stage curtain are advertisements of the wares of Hester Street or portraits of the "star" actors. On the programmes and circulars distributed in the audience are sometimes amusing announcements of coming attractions or lyric praise of the "stars." Poetry is not infrequent, an example of which, literally translated, is:

Labor, ye stars, as ye will,
Ye cannot equal the artist;
In the garden of art ye shall not flourish;
Ye can never achieve his fame.
Can you play *Hamlet* like him?
The *Wild King*, or the *Huguenots*?
Are you gifted with feeling
So much as to imitate him like a shadow?
Your fame rests on the pen;
On the show-cards your flight is high;
But on the stage every one can see
How your greatness turns to ashes,
Tomashevsky! Artist great!
No praise is good enough for you;
Every one remains your ardent friend.
Of all the stars you remain the king.

You seek no tricks, no false quibbles;
One sees Truth itself playing.
Your appearance is godly to us;
Every movement is full of grace;
Pleasing is your every gesture;
Sugar-sweet your every turn;
You remain the King of the Stage;
Everything falls to your feet.

On the playboards outside the theatre, containing usually the portrait of a star, are also lyric and enthusiastic announcements. Thus, on the return of the great Adler, who had been ill, it was announced on the boards that "the splendid eagle has spread his wings again."

The Yiddish actors, as may be inferred from the verses quoted, take themselves with peculiar seriousness, justified by the enthusiasm, almost worship, with which they are regarded by the people. Many a poor Jew, man or girl, who makes no more than $10 a week in the sweat-shop, will spend $5 of it on the theatre, which is practically the only amusement of the Ghetto Jew. He has not the loafing and sporting instincts of the poor Christian, and spends his money for the theatre rather than for drink. It is not only to see the play that the poor Jew goes to the theatre. It is to see his friends and the actors. With these latter he, and more frequently she, try in every way to make acquaintance, but commonly are compelled to adore at a distance. They love the songs that are heard on the stage, and for these the demand is so great that a certain bookshop on the east side makes a specialty of publishing them. . . .

. . . . .

The plays at these theatres vary in a general way with the varying audiences of which I have spoken above. The thinking socialists naturally select a less violent play than the comparatively illogical anarchists. Societies of relatively conservative Jews desire a historical play in which the religious Hebrew in relation to the persecuting Christian is put in pathetic and melodramatic situations. There are a very large number of "culture" pieces produced, which, roughly speaking, are plays in which the difference between the Jew of one generation and the next is dramatically portrayed. The pathos or tragedy involved in differences of faith and "point of view" between the old rabbi and his more enlightened children is expressed in many historical plays of the general character of *Uriel Acosta,* tho in less lasting form. Such plays, however, are called "historical plunder" by that very up-to-date element of the intellectual Ghetto which is dominated by the Russian spirit of realism. It is the demand of these fierce realists that of late years has produced a supply of theatrical productions attempting to present a faithful picture of the actual conditions of life. Permeating all these kinds of plays is the amusement instinct pure and simple. For the benefit of the crowd of ignorant people grotesque humor, popular songs, vaudeville tricks, are inserted everywhere.

Of these plays the realistic are of the most value, for they often give the actual Ghetto life with surprising strength and fidelity. The past three years have been their great seasons, and have developed a large crop of new playwrights, mainly journalists who write miscellaneous articles for the east side newspapers. Jacob Gordin . . . has been writing plays for several years, and was the first realistic playwright; he remains the strongest and most prominent in this kind of play. . . .

When we turn to Jacob Gordin's plays, to other plays of similar character and to the audiences to which they specifically appeal, we have realism worked out consciously in art, the desire to express life as it is, and at the same time the frequent expression of revolt against the reality of things, and particularly against the actual system of society. Consequently the "problem" play has its representation in the Ghetto. It presents the hideous conditions of life in the Ghetto—the poverty, the sordid constant reference to money, the immediate sensuality, the jocular callousness—and underlying the mere statement of the facts an intellectual and passionate revolt.

7 / A LOVER OF THE CITY

Despite the drawbacks, hardships, even misery of the city, Americans were deserting the land in increasing numbers to take their chances in the urban setting. "Mr. Dooley," the sagacious Chicago saloonkeeper, here tells some of the reasons for this migration.

"Where's Dorsey, the plumber, these days?" asked Mr. Hennessy.

"Have n't ye heerd?" said Mr. Dooley. "Dorsey's become a counthry squire. He 's landed gintry, like me folks in th' ol' dart. He lives out among th' bur-rds an' th' bugs, in a house that looks like a cuckoo clock. In an hour or two ye 'll see him go by to catch the five five. He won't catch it because there ain't anny five five. Th' la-ad that makes up th' time-table found las' week that if he did n't get away arlier he cudden't take his girl f'r a buggy ride an' he 's changed th' five five to four forty-eight. Dorsey will wait f'r th' six siven an' he 'll find that it don't stop at Paradise Manor where he lives on Saturdahs an' Winsdahs except Fridahs in Lent. He 'll get home at iliven o'clock an' if his wife 's f'rgot to lave th' lanthern in th' deepo, he 'll crawl up to th' house on his hands an' knees. I see him las' night in at th' dhrug sthore buyin' ile iv peppermint f'r his face. ' 'T is a gran' life in th' counthry,' says he, 'far' he says, 'fr'm th' madding crowd,' says he. 'Ye have no idee,' he says, 'how good it makes a man feel,' he says, 'to escape th' dust an' grime iv th' city,' he says, 'an' watch th' squrls at play,' he says. 'Whin I walk in me own garden,' he says, 'an' see th' viggytables comin' up, I hope, an' hear me own cow lowin' at th' gate iv th' fence,' he says, 'I f'rget,' he says, 'that they'se such a thing as a jint to be wiped or

SOURCE: Finley Peter Dunne, "The City As a Summer Resort," *Mr. Dooley's Opinions* (New York and London: Harper and Brothers, 1906), pp. 45–51.

a sink to be repaired,' he says. He had a box iv viggytables an' a can iv condensed milk undher his arm. 'Th' wife is goin' away nex' week,' he says, 'do ye come out an' spind a few days with me,' he says. 'Not while I have th' strenth to stay here,' says I. 'Well,' he says, 'maybe,' he says, 'I 'll r-run in an' see ye,' he says. 'Is there annything goin' on at th' theaytres?' he says.

"I wanst spint a night in th' counthry, Hinnissy. 'T was whin Hogan had his villa out near th' river. 'T was called a villa to distinguish it fr'm a house. If 't was a little bigger 't wud be big enough f'r th' hens an' if 't was a little smaller, 't wud be small enough f'r a dog. It looked as if 't was made with a scroll saw, but Hogan mannyfacthered it himself out iv a design in th' pa-aper. 'How to make a counthry home on wan thousan' dollars. Puzzle: find th' money.' Hogan kidnaped me wan afthernoon an' took me out there in time to go to bed. He boosted me up a laddher into a bedroom adjinin' th' roof. 'I hope,' says I, 'I'm not discommodin' th' pigeons,' I says. 'There ain't anny pigeons here,' says he. 'What's that?' says I. 'That's a mosquito,' says he. 'I thought ye didn't have anny here,' says I. ' 'Tis th' first wan I've seen,' says he, whackin' himsilf on th' back iv th' neck. 'I got ye that time, assassin,' he says hurlin' th' remains to th' ground. 'They on'y come,' he says, 'afther a heavy rain or a heavy dhry spell,' he says, 'or whin they'se a little rain,' he says, 'followed be some dhryness,' he says. 'Yet must n't mind thim,' he says. 'A mosquito on'y lives f'r a day,' he says. ' 'Tis a short life an' a merry wan,' says I. 'Do they die iv indigisthion?' I says. So he fell down through th' thrap dure an' left me alone.

"Well, I said me prayers an' got into bed an' lay there, thinkin' iv me past life an' wondherin if th' house was on fire. 'T was warrum, Hinnissy. I'll not deny it. Th' roof was near enough to me that I cud smell th' shingles an' th' sun had been rollin' on it all day long an' though it had gone away, it'd left a ray or two to keep th' place. But I'm a survivor iv th' gr-reat fire an' I often go down to th' rollin' mills an' besides, mind ye, I'm iv that turn iv mind that whin 't is hot I say 't is hot an' lave it go at that. So I whispers to mesilf, 'I'll dhrop off,' I says, 'into a peaceful slumber,' I says, 'like th' healthy ploughboy that I am,' says I.

An' I counted as far as I knew how an' conducted a flock iv sheep in a steeple chase an' I'd just begun f'r to wondher how th' las' thing I thought iv came into me head, whin a dog started to howl in th' yard. They was a frind iv this dog in th' nex' house that answered him an' they had a long chat. Some other dogs butted in to be companionnable. I heerd Hogan rollin' in bed an' thin I heerd him goin' out to get a dhrink iv wather. He thripped over a chair befure he lighted a match to look at th' clock. It seemed like an hour befure he got back to bed. Be this time, th' dogs was tired an' I was thinkin' I'd take a nap whin a bunch iv crickets undher me windows begun f'r to discoorse. I've heerd iv th' crickets on th' hearth, Hinnissy, an' I used to think they were all th' money, but anny time they get on me hearth I buy me a pound iv insect powdher. I'd rather have a pianola on th' hearth anny day, an' Gawd save me fr'm that! An' so 't was dogs an' mosquitos an' crickets an' mosquitos an' a screech owl an' mosquitos an' a whip-poor-will an' mosquitos an' cocks beginnin' to crow at two in th' mornin' an' mosquitos, so that whin th' sun bounced up an' punched me in th' eye at four, I knew what th' thruth is, that th' counthry is th' noisiest place in th' wurruld. Mind ye, there's a roar in th' city, but in th' counthry th' noises beats on ye'er ear like carpet tacks bein' dhriven into th' dhrum. Between th' chirp iv a cricket an' th' chirp iv th' hammer at th' mills, I'll take th' hammer. I can go to sleep in a boiler shop but I spint th' rest iv that night at Hogan's settin' in th' bath tub.

"I saw him in th' mornin' at breakfast. We had canned peaches an' condinsed milk. 'Ye have ye'er valise,' says he. 'Are n't ye goin' to stay out?' 'I am not,' says I. 'Whin th' first rattler goes by ye 'll see me on th' platform fleein' th' peace an' quite iv th' counthry, f'r th' turmoil an' heat,' I says, 'an' food iv a gr-reat city,' I says. 'Stay on th' farm,' says I. 'Commune,' I says, 'with nature,' I says. 'Enjoy,' I says, 'th' simple rustic life iv th' merry farmer boy that goes whistlin' to his wurruk befure breakfast,' says I. 'But I must go back,' I says, 'to th' city,' I says, 'where there is nawthin' to eat but what ye want an' nawthin' to dhrink but what ye can buy,' I says. 'Where th' dust is laid be th' sprinklin' cart, where th' ice-man comes reg'lar an' th' roof garden is in bloom an' ye're waked not be th' sun but be th' milkman,' I says. 'I want to be near a doctor whin I'm sick an' near eatable food whin I 'm hungry, an' where I can put me hand out early in th' mornin' an' hook in a newspaper,' says I. 'Th' city,' says I, 'is th' on'y summer resort f'r a man that has iver lived in th' city,' I says. An' so I come in.

" 'T is this way, Hinnissy, th' counthry was all right whin we was young and hearty, befure we become enfeebled with luxuries, d' ye mind. 'T was all right whin we cud shtand it. But we're not so sthrong as we was. We 're diff'rent men, Hinnissy. Ye may say, as Hogan does, that we 're ladin' an artificyal life but, be Hivins, ye might as well tell me I ought to be paradin' up an' down a hillside in a suit iv skins, shootin' th' antylope an' th' moose, be gorry, an' livin' in a cave as to make me believe I ought to get along without sthreet cars an' ilicthric lights an' illyvators an' sody wather an' ice. 'We ought to live where all th' good things iv life comes fr'm,' says Hogan. 'No,' says I. 'Th' place to live in is where all th' good things iv life goes to.' Ivrything that's worth havin' goes to th' city; th' counthry takes what's left. Ivrything that's worth havin' goes to th' city an' is iced. Th' cream comes in an' th' skim-milk stays; th' sunburnt viggytables is consumed be th' hearty farmer boy an' I go down to Callaghan's store an' ate th' sunny half iv a peach. Th' farmer boy sells what he has f'r money an' I get th' money back whin he comes to town in th' winther to see th' exposition. They give us th' products iv th' sile an' we give thim cottage organs an' knock-out dhrops, an' they think they've broke even. Don't lave annywan con-vince ye th' counthry's th' place to live, but don't spread th' news yet f'r awhile. I'm goin' to advertise 'Dooleyville be-th' river. Within six siconds iv sthreet cars an' railway thrains an' aisy reach iv th' theaytres an' ambulances. Spind th' summer far fr'm th' busy haunts iv th' fly an' th' bug be th' side iv th' purlin' ice wagon.' I 'll do it, I tell ye. I 'll organ-ize excursions an' I 'll have th' poor iv th' counthry in here settin' on th' cool steps an' passin' th' can fr'm hand to hand; I 'll take thim to th' ball-game an' th' theaytre; I 'll lave thim sleep till breakfast time an'

I' ll sind thim back to their overcrowded homes to dhream iv th' happy life in town. I will so."

"I'm glad to hear ye say that," said Mr. Hennessy. "I wanted to go out to th' counthry but I can't unless I sthrike."

"That's why I said it," replied Mr. Dooley.

PART II

Currents of Reform

By the second decade of the century, urban Americans were fully absorbed in dreams of reform and efforts to make those dreams come true. As a result of natural crises (such as the Galveston Flood of 1901) and the exposés of the muckrakers, the voters in one city after another seized upon stratagems which, they were assured, would not only keep the rascals out, but would ensure efficient public service. But some of the more thoughtful critics of the city realized that mere juggling of the political apparatus would not solve the growing problems of the urban communities. The continuing surge of immigration into the cities from Europe and the countryside, the rapid spread of factory sprawl, and the persistent growth of the slums were clear evidence, to those who would look, that social and economic reforms were no less important to the city than political reform.

Governmental change, however, was the preoccupation of most urban reformers. The civil service reform movement had spread from its concern with the federal bureaucracy to the officials of the states and the cities. Citizens were urged to apply objective professional standards even to candidates for public office (Selection 8). The zeal for professionalism led to such devices as the city manager plan. Like most reforms, however, this one often ran into political realities; city managers, too, had to learn how to play politics (Selection 9).

In a few places the voters simply refused to continue the Tweedledum-Tweedledee game of choosing between Republicans and Democrats and put Socialists into mayors' chairs. Generally, the new incumbents turned out to be reformers rather than revolutionaries; rarely did they hold office more than a single term (Selection 10).

It had become a commonplace that as new arrivals learned to accept the general culture, language, and attitudes, they would in turn be accepted by the established community and absorbed by it. On this belief rested many of the hopes for improving the cities. This process of acculturation particularly interested those social workers who labored among the immigrant poor. Some of the leaders of this new profession hoped that through careful study of various neighborhoods and districts they could prepare plans to cure the cities' ills (Selection 11). One ethnic group, however, despite its undoubted Americanism, was neither accepted nor absorbed by the larger community. When the needs of industry during the First World War brought many Southern Negroes to Northern industrial cities, racial strife belied the grand objective of making the world safe for democracy (Selection 12).

8 / HOW TO CHOOSE AN HONEST MAYOR

How civil service reform principles might be applied to the election of public officials is suggested by Charles J. Bonaparte, philanthropist, civil service reformer, and one-time Attorney General of the United States. It is interesting to note that in his final paragraph the author makes an oblique reference to the ultimate failure of his illustrious (collateral) ancestor.

It has been often said that, "to secure good city government, we must purify our city politics," and I think this saying contains a large measure of truth. . . . When we speak of "pure politics," we mean politics controlled and guided by sincere, scrupulous and unselfish men; the politics of any community can be "purified" only by leading such men to engage in them and driving other men out of them; and each of us aids in the "purifying" process when he tries to render a political career attractive to our best citizens, and does what he can to make the worst gain a living otherwise.

To this end, a first step, and a very long one (so long that it may go far towards making any second step needless), will be the thoroughgoing, practical application of the principles of civil service reform in our municipal government. Here, however, we may well pause a moment to see if we fully understand what "civil service reform" means; and there is the more reason to do this because I believe no little confusion of thought exists on this subject, even among those in general sympathy with the movement for good government and pure politics, and that to this fact much of the prejudice and apathy encountered by the advocates

SOURCE: Charles J. Bonaparte, "Municipal Civil Service Reform," *National Municipal Review,* I (April, 1912), 252–56. Reprinted by permission.

of civil service reform can be, more or less directly, traced; whatever reasonable doubt may exist as to whether the American people really want civil service reform arises only from a difference of opinion, or rather a misapprehension, as to what civil service reform means. In truth, many persons imagine that civil service reform, as a system, requires the selection of all public officers by competitive examination, or else their retention in office during good behavior, and associate with it no other idea whatsoever beyond these two. Undoubtedly, in many cases the principles of the reform can be best applied practically to the choice of public servants by adopting a method of appointment which leaves no room for favoritism, and making continued employment and promotion depend, and depend only, upon proved efficiency and fidelity; but there is room for these principles, however the officer is chosen and however long or short, certain or uncertain may be his term. These principles, or, to speak more accurately, for they can all be reduced to one, this principle, is simply that every public office exists for the sole benefit of the people and cannot be maintained, consistently with the fundamental theory of our government, in any measure or under any circumstances for the benefit of the individual holding such office for the time being, or of any other individual or organization, and, therefore, every office ought to be filled with a sole regard to the fitness of the incumbent to so discharge its duties as to fulfil those ends which the people sought when they created it and seek when they pay for its maintenance.

When a city is about to choose its principal administrative officer how can it apply the principles of civil service reform in this choice? . . .

. . . . .

The constitution and present laws of Maryland contain a virtual advertisement, published every four years, requesting those anxious for a . . . job in Baltimore to file applications with the supervisors of elections; which applications, each fourth year, are passed upon by the legal voters of the city on the Tuesday after the first Monday of May. Two of these applicants, known respectively as the Democratic and Republican nominees, are allowed to obtain a recommendation for the place of a somewhat peculiar character from certain classes of these voters on the like day in April, and, although the law gives these two individuals no material advantage over any other in the competition, experience teaches us that one or the other of them will be certainly chosen.

Some ten or eleven years ago, at a meeting of the National Civil Service Reform League held in New York, Theodore Roosevelt, then governor of the state, narrated an incident of his service as United States civil service commissioner. A request had been made to exempt from the competitive examinations customs officers on the Rio Grande frontier, because their duties required them to watch and often chase and arrest a class of smugglers decidedly "quick on the trigger" themselves and who needed officers no less "quick on the trigger" to deal with them. Mr. Roosevelt thereupon induced his colleagues to refuse the desired exemption, but to direct a competitive examination of candidates for these positions in shooting at a mark, and to credit those men who made good scores with a high percentage in their rating.

A speaker who followed him at the meeting suggested that, if the candidates, instead of using a target, had been allowed to shoot at each other, the results of this competition might have been even more satisfactory and decisive, not to mention the incidental advantages that there could be then no room for complaint as to the fairness of the marks or need for preserving the records. It may seem, at first sight, that a system of competition somewhat similar in consequences to the one thus proposed has been provided for applicants for our Baltimore mayoralty; but, as these are permitted only to kill off each other politically, instead of physically, the voters, first of the two leading parties, afterwards of the entire electorate, must, after all, bear the responsibility of deciding the contest; and a few words as to the principles on which they ought to decide it may not be untimely or wholly superfluous.

In the first place, they must remember that the mayor's obvious and most urgent duty is to frustrate the designs and foil the plots of those who correspond in mischievous activity to the Rio

Grande smugglers. These people always propose to plunder and discredit the city in future as they have too often done, with great profit to themselves, in the past; if they fail in this purpose, it will not be for want of trying, and, although the mayor (perhaps unfortunately), is not expected, or even permitted, to "wing" a grafter or put a "potshot" into a boss, whenever he runs across an active member of one or the other fraternity, he needs no less vigilance and no less resolution to deal with such gentry as they should be dealt with. If he comes before the examining board, consisting in my native city of 120,000, or thereabouts, which must finally pass on his claims, bearing a certificate from the very people it will be his business as mayor to watch and fight, a certificate saying, in substance, that he suits them "down to the ground," and that they will do all they can, by hook or by crook, to get him the job he seeks, this endorsement ought to affect his chances as much as a glowing eulogy from the smugglers would have tended to promote the choice of a revenue officer. . . .

Secondly, in the rating of these would-be public servants a very large percentage should be given to the applicant's record in making himself obnoxious to evil-doers and protecting the people's interest while holding other positions of public trust. Especially is he entitled to high credit if he has earned the ill-will of those who make their livelihood and gain actual or comparative wealth by preying on the public and particularly on his municipality. On the other hand, if his record as a trustee of the public is one of unbroken harmony with those who grow richer by making his *cetteux que trustent* poorer, this fact ought to lower his average very perceptibly: a watchdog particularly friendly with wolves is not one to put on guard at the sheepfold.

Thirdly, it will be well to conduct a brief written examination as to the candidate's views about pending measures of great moment to his community, and desirable, most of all, to get them down in black and white as to what they severally think of any such measures which tend to prevent the use of patronage as "spoils." Of course, it is possible that one may say he approves a proposal of this nature when his record shows, or tends strongly to show, that he speaks falsely; but, although possible, this is decidedly improbable; the chances are many to one that a man who doesn't wish to see it a law or mean to aid in its enactment, will try to avoid speaking of it at all; or, if compelled to say something, will shuffle and quibble, will say he hasn't had time to study its provisions carefully, or promise to support it with some unspecified amendments.

Fourthly and finally, we must remember that, although in many cities endorsements from the "affiliated" voters of the two great national parties, in the form of "nominations" for the office, are given, not by law, but by our political customs a very great weight in the determination of this question, these customs are by no means commendable, and, while it is overwhelmingly probable that in nine cases out of ten our choice will be practically one between the Democratic and the Republican nominees, we ought to have no more hesitancy in voting against the one of these who may agree with us as to the tariff, or any other national issue, if his competitor promises to make a better mayor, than we should have, under the like circumstances, in voting against a candidate who shared our religious belief. . . .

. . . . .

. . . The points of difference between Republicanism and Democracy have very much to do with a man's fitness to be a president or a congressman, but they also have nothing or next to nothing in the world to do with his fitness to be a mayor or a city comptroller or a president of the city council.

We say these things, not because we are indifferent to politics, but because we see how little, how very little national politics have properly to do with municipal officers. It is related that when General Bourmont was presented to Blücher, the latter, a man of violent prejudices but a thorough soldier, indicated his professional contempt for the deserter so unmistakably as to embarrass his more diplomatic staff. One of them, thinking it might please his commander, pointed out the enormous white cockade which Bourmont ostentatiously wore in proof of devotion to Legitimist principles. "Bah," said the old Field Marshal; "that doesn't matter. A blackguard stays a blackguard, however you label him." When the voters of a great American city clearly understand that "labeling" the tool of a corrupt "ring" the nominee of a great party leaves him just what he was before, and doesn't change in the least their duty as voters, when that time shall come then they will have a good mayor.

9 / STANDARDS AND ETHICS OF THE CITY MANAGER

A professional reformer and secretary of the National Short Ballot Organization, Richard S. Childs, suggests to professional city administrators just how the city manager should comport himself and do his job.

Professional Standards

The first question before the house is, "What is a city manager?" It is obvious that everybody who calls himself a city manager is not necessarily a real one. It is obvious that the title of city manager conferred upon a given office in a city charter does not necessarily make the incumbent really a city manager or entitle him to admission into a scrupulous city managers' association as a member of the profession in full standing.

A certain city in Tennessee, for example, had an officer known as the city commissioner, who had considerable work to do in connection with public works. The council passed a resolution which ran substantially as follows:

Whereas it is getting to be the fashion for up to date cities to have city managers, and,

source: Richard S. Childs, "Professional Standards and Professional Ethics in the New Profession of City Manager," *National Municipal Review,* V (April, 1916), 195–201. Reprinted by permission.

WHEREAS it will make —— City look like an up to date city to have a city manager,

Therefore, be it resolved, that the title of the present city commissioner be changed to city manager.

To be sure that officer had little or no appointive power, was completely excluded from some of the most important city departments, and despite his title, could not in any sense assume to "manage" the city, but the council nevertheless forwarded a copy of the resolution to the Short Ballot Organization and evidently expected to be listed thenceforth among commission manager cities, and no doubt the city manager of that town considers himself a full-fledged city manager,

Titusville, Pa., has a so-called city manager, but he is only the manager of part of the departments. The police department, for example, is not under his charge at all. He is in reality simply a superintendent of public works. In San Diego, Cal., likewise, the powers of the city manager and the experience and training which he is getting are very incomplete.

Another set of cases is the cities which have a city manager subject to divided responsibility under a mayor and council of the old-fashioned type. Such cities have city managers, but not the commission-manager plan. In some cases the manager is appointed by the mayor. Such a framework of government, lacking so many of the basic principles which are essential to good government in the long run, is very liable to get into trouble from time to time and to give to the true commission-manager plan and to city managers, an undeserved bad name.

Should not the City Managers' Association, anxious to establish high and sound standards for membership in the new profession, exclude such managers, or set them apart as being not quite the real thing?

Again, what is a "city"? Shall the future manager of Podunk (pop. 900) stand on a professional parity with the future city manager of Boston?

Here's another teaser. Some commission manager charters require the manager to be chosen from among local talent. This provision denies the existence of the profession and in effect insists that the manager must be an amateur. City managers chosen under that provincial limitation will not in the long run be an ornament to the profession. Shall such a city be encouraged to believe that it has the whole genuine modern plan of government?

The City Managers' Association has already adopted a definition of city manager and admits to its membership "any one who is the administrative head of the city appointed by its legislative body." At the present stage of development this rather easy-going definition is acceptable, for of course there are so few city managers in the country at present that it would be difficult otherwise to make up a satisfactory membership list. However, it seems to me that a stricter standard will eventually be necessary. . . .

. . . . .

Professional Ethics

A city manager who does not frequently know better than the people of the town or the commissioners what is good for them is a pretty poor city manager, but the people may not want what is good for them and it is not the city manager's business to jam it down their throats. No doubt there are towns where on a clear cut referendum the electorate would be likely to vote that all administrative offices, large or small, must be held by Republicans. The city manager knows better, but should he appoint a Democrat? How is he to determine whether or not he may venture to do it? The charter provides a guide for him. If a certain five or seven local citizens who have been elected for that very purpose of serving as fair samples of the ignorance and prejudices of the town, permit him to appoint a Democrat and will take the responsibility, then and not otherwise he may go ahead and do so.

The city manager is not called in to reform the city—that is the work for its citizens. He is called in to give as good an administration as he can persuade the commission to stand for. He may yearn to go further, to give them single tax, or strict law enforcement, a closed and dry Sunday, an efficient full rate assessment system, a non-political set of appointments, a less gaudy lighting of Main street, or a wholesome water supply, but if he cannot make these things seem worth while to the commissioners, he must stay his hand and bide his time.

He is the servant of the people first and always, but he has no authority to seek or interpret orders from the people direct—only through the commission. Suppose in his opinion the commission distorts those orders and instructs him to act counter to the popular wish? Is it his job to obey, provided no moral turpitude or deception is involved?

Take the case of R. C. Horne, ex-city manager of Beaufort, S. C. He had a brief dime-novel career there involving risk of his life and his story of his adventures and discoveries in that backward little burg would make a most enlivening contribution to the literature of the commission-manager movement. He undertook to reform the town in spite of the commissioners. Certain features of the tax laws had never been enforced with the result that numerous property owners in the town were, technically at least, heavily in arrears. He took it upon himself to revive these dead letter laws and made a sudden attack upon the leading bank, the president and cashier of which constituted two of his three commissioners, with a policeman, a warrant and a demand for $10,000 of back taxes. So there was a fight, a recall election and a political upheaval in which he became the popular leader of the so-called Horne forces. Incidentally, of course, he lost his job and was supplanted by another manager of different disposition.

Query—Did Horne do right?

I say it was right enough if he felt like doing it, but quite outside of his profession. If he had been mayor of that town the whole fight would have been within his clear field of duty. But he was not mayor—he was city manager. He stepped out of his profession, just as much as did the local physician and the local lawyer who helped him. He was frankly insubordinate. He took what was for one in his position a disorderly way to rectify a wrong. The orderly way would have been to present a formal proposal to a public meeting of the commission explaining openly and clearly the situation as he saw it. The commission would have to find an excuse for turning him down and would do so. The manager would then have his personal record clear. Unofficially he could privately call the attention of some of the local citizens to the incident and even wink in doing so, thus being personally disloyal, but not officially disloyal, to the commissioners who have no right to expect him to keep secrets for them. If a newspaper asks for an interview, he may officially restate the facts of the case, offering no opinions. Then it is up to local citizens to start something. Such a method is slower and less sensational. In some cases it would be less efficacious, in others more so. At any rate it is, I think, the professional way. . . .

Here is another case—Phoenix, Arizona. Manager Farrish, I understand, administered the town according to his ideals which were stricter than those of the commissioners. He demanded efficiency and economy of his subordinates and removed some politicians from the city service. The commission said "have a heart," but he kept going. He lost his job and the town was much wrought up about it for a time.

My theory of what should have been done in this case is this: When Manager Farrish had been given reason to think that his energy in kicking out politicians from the municipal service was distasteful to his superiors, he should have brought up the next case at the next public commission meeting saying "Mr. John Republican, superintendent of the water works, does not report for duty on Mondays, takes a great deal of time off during the week, neglects his inspection of the reservoirs, and continued admonition has been ineffective. I feel that the good of the service requires his removal and unless the commission objects, I will put in a new man there."

That brings it out in the open. If the commission wants to take the responsibility of standing up for Mr. John Republican, let it do so. It is the best judge of what the people of the town will like. If the commission openly insists on "having a heart," it is quite likely that the people in the town who consider such a thing outrageous will be found to be a minority. The manager, of course, could have simply removed John Republican, knowing that it would make the commissioners mad even if they did not dare say anything publicly about it—I take it that that is about what Farrish did do—but thereby the manager exceeds his true function. . . .

It is not the city manager's function to govern, but only to administer. The occasional manager who favors fixed definite tenure and power to defy the commission fails to comprehend the higher aspects of his job. It is not his function to blow into town and immediately implant in city hall all the ideals of the bureau of municipal research from which he graduated. . . . His function is only to give as good an administration as the commission will take responsibility for. In a town that elects a machine-controlled bunch of political puppets, the manager must go slow and cautiously and be content with getting ready to do very much better as soon as the town is in a mood to elect a better commission.

Good government that comes to a town, unasked and unwelcomed, will be unstable and transitory. Reform that endures must be built up laboriously, piece by piece, upon a firm basis of popular sympathy and consent.

10 / SOCIALISM IN SCHENECTADY

Schenectady, New York, a moderate-sized industrial city dominated by the General Electric Company, briefly tried a Socialist administration. Mayor George R. Lunn, a Protestant minister whose motivation was the Social Gospel rather than Marxism, led the experiment. Louis Heaton Fink, an observer of the reform scene, reports on the early accomplishments of the Socialists.

From New York to San Francisco, gesticulating street orators urge Schenectady as proof of successful Socialism. What has really been done in that little industrial city on the banks of the Mohawk? How does Socialist administration differ from any other?

When I came upon Walter Kruesi, Commissioner of Charities, he was sweeping out the municipal store in the basement of City Hall Annex. "We are a little short-handed to-day," he remarked, and went on with the job. The floor swept, we started upstairs. On the way we met an Italian woman with a mesh bag. "I came for some groceries," she said. "You are half an hour late, and the store is locked," said the Commissioner; "however, come on." He turned back, opened the store, and filled the mesh bag, which seemed capable of indefinite expansion. He was not cross or hurried, but suggested olive oil and macaroni when his customer had exhausted her wants.

Many of the callers in the Mayor's office were workmen in overalls. As I was talking with Mayor George R. Lunn, the

SOURCE: Louis Heaton Fink, "Socialism on Trial," *The Outlook*, CV (November 1, 1913), 489–94.

janitor, brush in hand, came in to discuss the policy of the administration.

The workman feels that the government is his as much as the shop-owner's, and that he is an important part of the body politic. City officials look upon their work as a mission. Democracy is real, not simulated.

Otherwise this Socialist administration and a Democratic or Republican administration are the same. Social revolution and common ownership of the tools of production are no nearer in Schenectady than in New York or Chicago or Key West.

The Big Things

The Socialist administration began January 1, 1912. I asked the Mayor what he considered the big things done. He answered:

(1) Solving the water problem.
(2) Increasing the pay of laborers.
(3) Establishing a garbage-disposal plant, and beginning the free collection of garbage and ashes.

Schenectady owns its water system, but in 1903 made a contract with the Schenectady Railway Company—now the Schenectady Illuminating Company—to pump for the city system. For several years the company and the city have been at odds, each claiming breach of contract. The city has failed to provide adequate storage, and the company has not established proper pumping facilities and maintained adequate pressure. The city was growing fast, and the situation became dangerous. On July 28, 1913, the Common Council ratified an agreement with the company, which promised to erect new pumps and release the city from all claims for damages, the city binding itself to build a twelve-million-gallon storage reservoir.

When the Socialists found themselves at the helm, laborers were paid $1.75 a day. One of the first acts of the new administration was to raise the pay to $2. Last spring another increase was made to $2.25. The city compels contractors on municipal work to pay the same wage, so that the average rate in all employments has been affected. Mayor Lunn says that labor is better paid in Schenectady than in any other city in the State.

Schenectady has never before made provision for disposal of garbage. The State Board of Health long ago ordered the city to build a disposal plant, but only now is the work under way. . . .

These are, in the eyes of the Mayor, the three "big things." There is nothing Socialistic about them. Any moderately progressive city would have done likewise. The remarkable thing is that these needs were not attended to years ago and that it was left to a chance Socialist administration to gain the credit for doing the obvious.

Schenectady has had a magic growth. In 1890 the population was 19,900; in 1900, 31,600; in 1910, 72,800; to-day it is close to 90,000. When the Socialists were put in power, the city was like an overgrown youth, man-size in knee pants. Streets, parks, schools, public conveniences—none of these had been cut to fit.

Twenty-five per cent of the public school pupils are on half time. Sixty-five per cent of the schools are overcrowded. In eight years the number of high school pupils has doubled, and there are not accommodations for them. Through a bond issue the Socialists have authorized the erection of schools to accommodate all pupils on full time.

Of parks and playgrounds there were one each on January 1, 1912. The sole park is the patch of green at the head of State Street. There are now ten playgrounds, adjacent to school buildings, all equipped and under competent supervision.

A City Plan and Park Commission has been appointed by the Mayor, consisting of one Socialist, Professor Charles P. Steinmetz, of Union College, who is also President of the Board of Education, three citizens who represent the political parties as well as the large industries of the city, and a woman physician. This board has prepared a plan for an ideal Schenectady of the future, and has recommended the purchase of three large parks with the proceeds of the $300,000 bond issue recently made for this purpose. One of these takes in the land along the river front, which is capable of being made into one of the finest public pleasure resorts in the country.

A central purchasing bureau has been established, which buys supplies in quantities for all departments, and has effected a saving estimated at thirty per cent.

Plans have been prepared for the market site purchased by the former administration. Buildings are to be erected with stores and stalls. The market should bring farmer and consumer face to face, and reduce the cost of food. Heretofore the market has been largely for the supply of stores and hotels.

Schenectady has this year joined Worcester, Los Angeles, Milwaukee, and other progressive cities in using schools and public buildings for polling-places. Fifteen public buildings (including the City Hall, fire-house, court-house, municipal lodging-house, and eleven school basements), one church, eleven booths, and three business buildings will be used.

. . . . .

The Health Service has had the attention of the entire administration. The Board of Public Welfare, which Helen Keller was to head, is modeled after a department of the same name in Kansas City; it has made many suggestions for more effective work. The number of health physicians has been increased from one to four. These doctors give free medical attention to any poor family. It is the aim of the Socialist to make medical attention free for all wage-earners a matter of right rather than charity. A milk station and a dental clinic have been established. A maternity and infancy nurse has been added to the health staff, and the force of school nurses increased. A free city dispensary has been started. A chemist has been engaged and rigid inspection of the milk and food supply is carried on.

. . . . .

The Mayor

The sparking-plug of the Socialist machine, the Mayor, is tall, thin, distinguished-looking; clean shaven, boyish, well dressed. He has an engaging smile. He runs rapidly over the scale from comic to serious and back again. He rams home his arguments with gestures, has a splendid voice and an eye that holds. Impetuous, full of fun, bubbling over with boyish enthusiasm, rushing pell-mell into some serious difficulty and smiling and bluffing his way out, courageous to a fault, by many considered the best orator in New York State, Mayor Lunn is a power to be reckoned with.

Few dime-novel heroes have had careers more varied than his.

He was called to Schenectady to become the pastor of the First Reformed Church, a wealthy parish, the front pews filled by the best families, many of them descendants from the old Dutch settlers. Lunn spoke from the shoulder. He preached Christian Socialism. Soon the church was in uproar. There was the Lunn or radical faction and the conservative element. Forced out, Lunn consolidated two dwindling congregations into the United People's Church. Here too a rift soon appeared. To this day the anti-Lunn faction uses the church at night and the Mayor preaches in the forenoon.

Lunn not only split open his churches, but the whole town took sides. To aid his fight Dr. Lunn purchased the "Citizen," a weekly paper, and made it the Socialist organ. This brought him a wider audience. He was nominated for Mayor in the fall of 1911; the people were disgusted with both old parties, the star of destiny twinkled, and, much to the surprise of every one, including the pastor-editor, he was elected.

"What are the big obstacles you have encountered?" I asked the Mayor.

"Whenever we try to do anything," he answered, "we run up against the Charter. It is an oak charter, fixed and immovable. It is, by all means, the one great obstacle we have had to overcome. Our second greatest trouble has been pettifogging politicians, the 'old guard.' They have done everything possible to block us. Take the matter of injunctions. My drawer is full of them. The wonder is that we have been able to do anything, hampered this way."

. . . . .

"Do you know," said the Mayor, with quiet earnestness, "they charge me with being against law? I am not. I believe in law. The more I see law abused, the more I believe in it. Law should be for the protection of the people, it should not be abused. It should be another name for justice. Law is the shell, justice is the kernel. It is the kernel that is alive, the shell is a mere covering. Sometimes it may be necessary to break the shell to give the kernel room to grow. Law should accommodate itself to justice."

From law he turned to Christianity.

"Christianity is service," mused the Mayor. "Often those who do not profess Christianity, because they do not understand its forms, are the best Christians. They are the servants of their fellows. Law and Christianity are the foundations of the Socialist State. We can't inaugurate Socialism here. No city or group of cities can do it. But we can show the people that Socialism is not dangerous. Why, many prophesied ruin for the city when we came into power. Instead, Schenectady has grown as never before."

. . . . .

Catholics in the Fold

Socialists and Catholics are supposed to be in a desperate fight for life—but not in Schenectady. There is little bitterness. The church authorities are friendly. From ten to fifteen per cent of the members of the Socialist party are Catholics. In New York, Chicago, and other large cities Socialists are largely foreigners. In Schenectady many native Americans have joined the ranks. The Socialists are as representative of the population of Schenectady as any other party.

Struggles within the Camp

All is not peaceful in the Socialist camp. There are radical Socialists and conservative Socialists. The revolutionary wing clamors for more drastic action, for warfare against capitalism, for government not by the chosen of the people, but by the party through its local branches and caucuses. The more conservative members, led by the Mayor, plead for orderly progress, for making a record in good government. . . .

Mayor Lunn has stood out firmly against party government. He has insisted that he be left free to act according to his conscience. He has refused to bow his head to caucus domination. When the Socialist party voted that officials must in all things follow the party vote, Dr. Lunn refused to pledge himself to this policy, but despite his bold stand was renominated almost unanimously.

The effect of the party on the administration is disputed. Some say that it has been a drag, threatening disaster through tyranny and meddling; others that it has been an inspiration to the officials—that the existence of a solid and powerful body watching every act and demanding more and yet more has forced the city officials to accomplish far greater results than would have been possible if they had been left alone. However that may be, we have not reached that point in America where we are willing to surrender the government of our cities to any party machine. The domination of a Socialist machine is likely to be as arrogant and as dangerous as that of any other party. We are trying to free our cities from party domination. It is that which has led us into the mire of graft and incompetence. The Socialists cannot go far if they keep candidates chosen by the people under leash and chain. So far party dictation has been held at bay; it must continue to be held at bay or Socialist rule in Schenectady will go to smash.

Socialists a Minority

Excepting so far as Socialism voices protest against the old order in politics, Schenectary is not a Socialist city. There are but 1,200 enrolled members of the party. Mayor Lunn received 6,536 votes out of a total of 15,357, running an even thousand ahead of the Democratic candidate, Charles H. Benedict. But almost two-thirds of these voters were Democrats and Republicans. The last

National election is a close indication of the real strength of the party. Debs polled 2,871 votes out of 13,477.

All three parties, Democratic, Republican, and Progressive, have fused to beat the Socialists. . . . Everything points to a repetition of the experience in Milwaukee, where, though the Socialist vote increased, yet, through fusion of all parties, Mayor Seidel was beaten. The re-election of Mayor Lunn seems impossible. . . .

11 / CHANGING TIDES

Two internationally famous settlement workers, Robert A. Woods and Albert J. Kennedy of Boston's South End House, studied "The Zone of Emergence," the area between suburbia and downtown where successive waves of immigrants underwent the metamorphosis into Americans. This survey, based on 1912 data, remained unpublished for fifty years.

A city is naturally round. In the Anglo Saxon world its nucleus is the "market," a downtown commercial and manufacturing quarter about which zone after zone is circlingly added as the population increases. The belt immediately about the business section, hemming it in, is given over to a circle of poor and crowded neighborhoods broken in one place by a downtown residential quarter illustrating wealth and social power. The outer edge of this inner belt usually marks the confines of the "old city." As additional territory is needed, the farms "beyond the

SOURCE: Robert A. Woods and Albert J. Kennedy, *The Zone of Emergence*, abridged and edited by Sam B. Warner, Jr. (Cambridge, Mass.: Harvard University Press, 1962), pp. 31–41. Reprinted by permission of the publishers.

walls" are invaded and disintegrated, or the adjacent towns are annexed. It sometimes happens that the land between the city proper and the suburbs, avoided in the outward movement, is neither city nor country, but gradually, by forward, sidewise, and even refluent pressure, intervening spaces are filled in, and the city completes its characteristic outline.

An oval peninsula, the town of Boston looks out over the water upon five jutting angles of land which run in toward it as a center: East and South Boston facing the outer harbor; Charlestown and Cambridge within; and Roxbury, with which it was once connected by an often overflowed isthmus or "neck," at the rear. As the city grew the downtown business quarter requisitioned the residential streets of the old town, and was itself later hemmed in by a series of congested tenement districts, broken only by the Back Bay. Beyond this inner belt, commonly known as the North, West, and South Ends, and the Back Bay, lie the ring of districts whose neglected story throws a deal of light upon the degree and method of progress which the city's immigrant peoples have been making.

A series of interlacing wave lines may be set forth to indicate the broad general and economic character of the belt as a whole. From the State House, which is the city's convenient geographical point of departure, the distance to the active center of each of these communities is nearly the same. Their downtown parts are near enough so that a considerable number of inhabitants walk to and from their work each day. Here runs the fire limit, the outer margin of tenement congestion within which wooden construction is not allowed, and beyond which the three-flat house is making rapid headway against the detached cottage. Here is the latitude of the standard wage of trade unionism. These various lines suggest a sort of beach up which people are struggling.

It is natural that public concern for urban conditions should first concentrate upon the need of the innermost tenement districts. Their situation brings them more or less continuously under the eye of the resourceful citizen, and their swarms of newly arrived immigrants continuously recreate the great drama of the building of the nation. Their colorful and dramatically staged misery makes a clear appeal to the city as a whole. This immediate and compelling challenge finally makes them a classic land of poverty. Unfortunately, in the minds of many citizens the clearly fixed field of civic responsibility and vision ends with these innermost tenement neighborhoods. Beyond is penumbra, in whose dim distance somewhere the average man believes the mass of the people live wholesomely in modified village isolation. . . . It is hoped that these pages will show that from an economic, a political, and a cultural point of view, the districts immediately between the old city and the suburbs constitute a single sociological fact with a sharply defined significance and appeal.

Two main causes have contributed to give the zone its special character. One of these is the development of rapid transit, the other is the growth and the changed character of the local industries. The chief concern of the people of these districts during many years was the vital one of getting into Boston. The main highways were laid out to this end, and in each community there was a time when the question of ferries and bridges most engaged the interest of the citizens. Once these improvements were secured the always vital problem of popular transportation came to the front. Each community rejoiced in its "hourlies" as the old stages were called. These were followed by the railways during the first half of the nineteenth century and each district was on the first station out of Boston. Horse cars were next provided, changing to the trolley and leading within the past decade to rapid transit by means of the elevated and the tunnel. The Elevated between Roxbury and Boston, the East Boston Tunnel, the Cambridge Tunnel, the East Cambridge Viaduct, and the projected tunnel through the upper end of South Boston and into Dorchester emphasize the emergence character of each community.

As the growth of commerce and industry makes increasing demands on the innermost portion of the city, those factories which require a considerable amount of space for their processes seek cheaper land on the outskirts of the city, and the older and more well-to-do inhabitants move away. The neighborhoods thus requisitioned naturally change character. It is this very tearing down of the community, however, which frees its more liberal conditions for the workers. Each of the districts under consideration was at one time a high-grade residential community. The American population retired before the inroads of the transportation companies and the factories, on the one hand, and the proximity of unskilled foreigners which the new industries called for on the other. Already, however, this same process is again being repeated. Further encroachments on the part of industry are now driving the Irish away, and their places are taken by more recent immigrants. . . .

Except in the case of the purely residential suburb close to a large city the local industries usually place the tone of the community. High grade industries attract and create a high grade population; and *vice versa.* Therefore the industrial fortunes of the communities we are considering are of the utmost importance. To a surprising degree, the industrial development of each one has proceeded on practically parallel lines. A period of rapid industrial growth based on peculiar local advantages of situation or on local enterprise; followed by a period of arrested development or even of industrial decline, lasting until 1900; followed again by a period of generous growth and upbuilding. The middle period of depression was brought on by a series of causes which affected the industry of the entire city. The decline of the iron and machine trades, the changes brought about by the formation of trust[s] and combines, and a series of labor difficulties together with a normal amount of poor organization and administration, and the failure of managerial ability in times of crisis, have all had their effect in changing the industrial character of the belt.

The present revival of industry within the zone is thoroughly sound, being based on nearness to the heart of Boston, on relatively cheap land, and on ease of transportation both by water and railways. The zone is peculiarly well situated for factories which carry on those services most necessary to maintain the physical well-being of the population, being strategically close to the downtown districts on the one hand, to the suburbs and the outlying country on the other. The characteristic industries include the railroad terminal service, the distribution of coal, wood, ice, milk; the preparation and manufacture of meat products, bread, crackers, soap; and the delivery of these goods and services over a wide range of territory. In addition to these most characteristic industries there is a wide variety of manufacture carried on in foundries, machine shops, piano factories, rubber works, cabinet making establishments and stone yards. Charlestown, East Boston, and South Boston, provide in their docks for a large seagoing and coast trade, and Roxbury and East Cambridge are reached from the harbor by schooner traffic in coal and lumber which struggles for its right of way against a series of drawbridges.

Though there are some exceptions, the neighborhoods of the Zone of Emergence impress one familiar with the downtown tenement communities as distinctly more habitable. The air is brighter, cleaner, and more vibrant; sunshine falls in floods rather than in narrow shafts; there is not so much dust and smoke; the streets are quieter; there is less congestion and more evident freedom of movement. These strikingly valuable advantages are found even in the worse portions of the community where the housing is in itself sometimes worse than that which is found in the downtown tenements. On the whole the housing of the zone is very much better than that of the inner belt. While there is a definite proportion of large tenements and poorly built houses, the majority of dwellings are three-family tenements or cottages, and practically all are detached with openings to the air in each room.

The total population of the zone (including Cambridge) was 297,772 in 1905 and 316,946 in 1910. The population of the Boston Wards 1 to 5; 13 to 15; 16 to 19 numbered 247,164 (1910) as over against 109,528 persons in Wards 6, 7, 8 and 9. The average density per acre in the zone is 56.24 as against 113.11 in the inner belt. Some notion of the growth of population will be seen from the fact that during the years 1901–1907, 105 new buildings of the first and second class (valued at $2,265,026) and 162 buildings of the third class (valued at $441,068) were erected yearly. In addition a very considerable amount of remodeling goes on constantly, whereby cottages and small dwellings are unfortunately turned into apartments for two and three families.

The men over twenty years of age are more than half unskilled or semi-skilled and their numbers, moreover, are nearly balanced by those of the skilled workmen and the clerks. Over sixty-five percent of the residence property of the zone is owned by those who reside on it, and this is the best possible index that can be given of the end that holds the imagination and galvanizes the powers of a large proportion of the population. Doubtless the greater share of this property is encumbered with mortgage, but it is an index of striving and accomplishment.

In national affiliation 73,755 or 24 percent of the population is American or third generation through foreign ancestry. 182,905 or 61 percent is English speaking immigrant (including provincials); 40,243 or 13 percent are non-English speaking immigrants of the first and second generation; 3,500 or 1 percent are Negroes. Eighty-six percent of the population uses English as its native tongue, and this great body of the population gives tone to the entire locality. Whatever may be true of the inner belt of the city, certainly the zone of emergence is predominantly Anglo Saxon.

On the side of the zone which touches the city, a few struggling relics of the native American forces remain. The rear guard of the city's American population is to be found on the suburban side of the zone.

Mingled with this American remnant and advancing on the whole with a more substantial momentum is a considerable body of Irish, Provincials, Italians, and Russian Jews. The Irish dominate; indeed the zone of emergence is the great Irish belt of the city. They entered the zone on the wake of the industries which drove out the American population. The departing Americans sold their property to the newcomers, who, at a single stroke, often thus secured living accommodations that represented a decided advance over any they had dreamt of previously. These cases where the environment served to advance family life are more than offset, however, by other cases in which the conditions presented in tenements remodeled from private dwellings tore it down. In its conditions of living, its social and political organization, and all those subtle qualities which give the tone of the community, the zone is second-generation Irish. . . .

. . . . .

Jews, Italians and Poles are found in each of the districts in the zone, and their colonies are an earnest of what may be expected of their fellows in the North and West Ends. The accomplishment of these peoples within a limited time has been very great, and argues much for their future as citizens.

. . . . .

The Protestant churches in the belt are far from vigorous, and, with one or two exceptions, are holding out against inevitable disintegration. The difficulty of keeping alive tends on the whole to make them uncooperative, and hence of less public influence than they might very reasonably be expected to have.

The recreation of the people is largely in the hands of commercial institutions. The Boston theatres and other amusement resorts attract large numbers of people in town. Each district of the zone has anywhere from one to half a dozen moving picture shows, and there are usually one or two halls for dances and parties. The public playgrounds care for a certain proportion of the children. It is interesting and significant that the school center movement finds its most successful exemplification in these localities.

12 / RACE RIOT IN THE NORTH

A few days after one of the worst race riots in American history, Oscar Leonard, a St. Louis social worker, visited the scene of the disorders. What he saw and learned of this unhappy episode is graphically described.

Two days before the nation was to celebrate the signing of the Declaration of Independence with its recognition that "all men are created free and equal" came the news that the East St. Louis Negroes were being slaughtered and their homes pillaged and burned by white Americans. East St. Louis, as all good St. Louisans wish to make clear, has nothing to do with the southwestern metropolis. It is an industrial town across the Mississippi. It is not located in Missouri. It is part of the state which gave us Abraham Lincoln. This circumstance made the "pogrom" upon the Negroes more tragic. They were being murdered mercilessly in a state which had fought for their freedom from slavery. They were forced to seek refuge and safety across the river in Missouri, which was a slave state at one time.

I just called the riot a "pogrom," the name by which Russian massacres of Jews has become known. Yet when I went to East St. Louis to view the sections where the riots had taken place, I was informed that the makers of Russian "pogroms" could learn a great deal from the American rioters. I went there in the company of a young Russian Jew, a sculptor, who had witnessed and bears the marks of more than one anti-Jewish riot in his native land. He told me when he viewed the blocks of burned houses that the Russian "Black Hundreds" could take lessons in pogrom-making from the whites of East St. Louis. The Russians at least, he said, gave the Jews a chance to run while they were trying

SOURCE: Oscar Leonard, "The East St. Louis Pogrom," *Survey*, XXXVIII (July 14, 1917), 331–33.

to murder them. The whites in East St. Louis fired the homes of black folk and either did not allow them to leave the burning houses or shot them the moment they dared attempt to escape the flames.

What is the reason for this terrible situation?

Fundamentally, the reason is purely economic. It is not that the white people in Illinois, or rather in East St. Louis, have any terrible hatred for the Negro. The two races go to the same schools. The laws of Illinois even permit intermarriage between whites and blacks. Negroes hold state, county and municipal offices. They own a great deal of property in the state and in the city where the riots took place. But being the most disinherited of men, Negroes at times work for lower wages than do whites. Some of them will not join labor unions and most of them would not be admitted if they cared to join.

This condition is extremely objectionable to the white workers with whom they compete for jobs. But this very fact makes the Negro laborer more attractive to employers who want labor at the cheapest possible terms. They favor any labor force that will not join unions, that will not strike, that will not make periodic demands for increased wages or shorter workdays. Such an element introduced into the community acts as a whip over the heads of the white workers. Employers know that. Laboring people are painfully aware of it. This is the main reason for the race antipathy in East St. Louis, as I judge from talking to business men, laborers, professional men and labor leaders.

East St. Louis is what Graham Romeyn Taylor called a "satellite city." It is not a city of homes, in the American acceptance of that term. It is a manufacturing town where industries locate because land is cheap, transportation facilities good, coal and water near and cheap. The many factories make the place unattractive for home-building. Capital goes there simply in search of dividends. It is not interested in the welfare of the city or of the workers who help make those dividends. Only those who must, live there. Those who can live in St. Louis, while working in East St. Louis, do so.

The result is that the city is run to suit the lowest political elements. The foreign laborers who were imported by the industries in East St. Louis know nothing of American standards. There is practically no social work being done in that city which boasts a population of 100,000 souls. Saloons are numerous and gambling dens abound. They run wide open. In fact, when Governor Folk closed the St. Louis saloons on Sunday, the city across the Mississippi reaped a rich harvest. Multitudes crossed Eads Bridge for their liquor in spite of the Illinois law which prohibited Sunday selling. The saloon element has been pretty much in control of the town, from all I can learn. I have these facts both from observation as a neighbor, and from good citizens, not necessarily prohibitionists. One can not visit East St. Louis without seeing at a glance that saloons are more numerous than schools and churches. That in itself would indicate how much control the liquor interests have over the city.

This, too, has helped bring about the situation which resulted in the massacre of Negroes both May 28 and July 2. The undesirable Negro element, like the undesirable white element, was used by self-seeking politicians. In order to be able to control that element the politicians had to make concessions. Evil dives were permitted. Lawless Negroes were protected. All too frequently the St. Louis papers reported outrages committed upon white women by Negroes in East St. Louis. There were robberies and stabbings and shootings of white men at frequent intervals. Yet criminals were not punished. They were "taken care of." This helped stir the ill will of the better element among the white population.

There were grumblings on the part of laboring people at the increased number of Negro workers who were coming into the city. But there was no open or pronounced hostility, although there were old scores to settle, from the days when some 2,500 white workers went on strike in the packing plants last summer and Negroes were imported to take their jobs. According to the former president of the Central Trades and Labor Union of East St. Louis, at that time Negroes were imported in box-cars and given the jobs held by striking white workers. When the strike was over about 800 of the Negro strike-breakers were retained and the white strikers lost those places.

. . . . .

The employers insist that they do not encourage Negro immigration and absolutely deny that they import Negroes. They insist that there are not enough white workers to take the jobs. They point to the fact that since the Negroes left East St. Louis, on July 2 and that entire week, four important industries have entirely shut down. When asked why it is that Negroes do come in such large numbers to East St. Louis they say that the lure of better wages than the South pays attracts them.

R. F. Rucker, superintendent of the aluminum ore plant, says that the employers were glad to employ Negroes when there were not enough white workers to fill the jobs. According to him, many of the white workers went east to take employment in munition factories where wages are higher. Some Negroes who had come voluntarily from the South were given their places. These men wrote home of the fine opportunities for employment at high wages and urged their friends to come to East St. Louis.

The fact remains that during a recent strike, when the government took possession of the factory, Negroes took the places of the strikers. This intensified the feeling against the race. The feeling was aggravated by the many lawless acts committed by the bad Negro element. Feeling began to run high so that on May 28 a meeting was called which was known as the "anti-race meeting."

In spite of the fact that the meeting was known in advance to be against the Negroes, permission was given for holding it in the city hall. I have these facts from a business man who was present. Mayor Mollman and the Board of Aldermen were among the 1,000 men who attended. Intemperate speeches were made and the last speaker is said to have hinted that unless the mayor and the city fathers did something to check the coming of Negroes, the people would take matters into their own hands. That night a race riot took place. The militia came and quelled the riot before it went too far.

Those who had attended the meeting, however, continued to agitate the idea that "East St. Louis must remain a white man's town." Feeling against the Negroes was stirred constantly. Here and there personal encounters between men of the two races took place. Sunday evening, July 1, a rumor was spread that the Negroes had gathered in one of their churches to plan revenge upon the white population. A number of policemen in charge of Detective Sergeant Coopedge drove over to the church. As they approached the place they were fired upon by Negroes and Coopedge was killed. The same night a policeman and two other white men were shot by Negroes.

These deeds acted as a match applied to powder. Monday morning it was apparent that there would be trouble. Mayor Mollman said he tried to prepare for it. East St. Louis has just thirty-six policemen. The mayor says that he spoke personally to them, urging them to do their duty. They were not inclined to interfere because their comrades had been shot. The deputy sheriffs felt the same way. Some militiamen were in town, but according to all accounts the militia fraternized with the white population. The mayor was urged to call up the governor and ask for reinforcements and for a declaration of martial law. He refused to do so. His opponents say that he had political reasons for his failure to act.

Be that as it may, the fact remains that through someone's negligence, black men and women and children were murdered wantonly. In the seven Negro districts of the city fires were started at the same time. Negroes were hanged and stoned and shot and kicked. White women and boys as well as men took part. A black skin was a death warrant on the streets of this Illinois city. How many black persons were killed will never be known.

. . . . .

It was a distressing sight to see block after block where peaceful homes had been located burned to the ground. The innocent suffered with the guilty. Thrifty black folk, who were doing their bit by raising vegetables, were murdered. I saw the ruins of their homes, into which had gone the labor and savings of years. The little thrift gardens had escaped the flames and the orderly rows where seeds had been planted gave the plots the appearance of miniature graveyards.

PART III

The Frenetic City

WITH the end of World War I, American cities entered upon an age of mingled boom and complacency. Growth was rarely questioned; it was generally regarded as an unmixed good. Nor were the new completely dominant goals and values of business doubted. Change, provided it was approved by business leaders, was identified with progress, and progress was good.

Even the emergence of the great Negro ghetto in Harlem was hailed as proof that the black man was at last coming out of the shadow of slavery (Selection 13). And if the improvement of municipal government seemed to falter a bit, the success of the Cincinnati reformers showed that businessmen—Republican businessmen, at that—could run cities better than anyone else (Selection 14). The best known study of an American community merely gave sociological affirmation to the obvious fact that it was the business leaders of every town who set the tone (Selection 15).

A few architects and city planners were not so sanguine about the virtue of uninhibited growth. Banded into the Regional Planning Association of America, they warned that the cities were becoming unmanageable (Selection 16) and that a better mixture of country and city was required if life was to remain worthwhile (Selection 17). Few Americans, however, heeded their cautioning and the "dinosaur" continued to grow.

One significant creation of the earlier period of urban history had been the recreation movement, which, by the 1920's, had reached respectable proportions. It had become sufficiently important to receive the accolade of respectability: the survey. Community after community engaged the services of a professional researcher to tell it what its recreational facilities were and what was wrong with them (Selection 18).

Finally, this period cannot be passed without a tribute to its most colorful aspect. So firmly established had the gangster become that, in Chicago, at any rate, he strove to maintain his city's reputation as a haven for culture (Selection 19).

13 / HARLEM IS HOPE

The distinguished Negro author and champion of the rights of his people, James Weldon Johnson, saw Harlem, in 1925, as a hopeful development in the Negro's efforts to enter the mainstream of American life. Compare this optimistic view with Selection 34.

In the history of New York, the significance of the name Harlem has changed from Dutch to Irish to Jewish to Negro. Of these changes, the last has come most swiftly. Throughout colored America, from Massachusetts to Mississippi, and across the continent to Los Angeles and Seattle, its name, which as late as fifteen years ago had scarcely been heard, now stands for the Negro metropolis. Harlem is indeed the great Mecca for the sight-seer, the pleasure-seeker, the curious, the adventurous, the enterprising, the ambitious and the talented of the whole Negro world; for the lure of it has reached down to every island of the Carib Sea and has penetrated even into Africa.

SOURCE: James Weldon Johnson, "The Making of Harlem," *The Survey: Graphic Number,* LIII (March 1, 1925), 635–39.

In the make-up of New York, Harlem is not merely a Negro colony or community, it is a city within a city, the greatest Negro city in the world. It is not a slum or a fringe, it is located in the heart of Manhattan and occupies one of the most beautiful and healthful sections of the city. It is not a "quarter" of dilapidated tenements, but is made up of new-law apartments and handsome dwellings, with well-paved and well-lighted streets. It has its own churches, social and civic centers, shops, theatres and other places of amusement. And it contains more Negroes to the square mile than any other spot on earth. A stranger who rides up magnificent Seventh Avenue on a bus or in an automobile must be struck with surprise at the transformation which takes place after he crosses One Hundred and Twenty-fifth Street. Beginning there, the population suddenly darkens and he rides through twenty-five solid blocks where the passers-by, the shoppers, those sitting in restaurants, coming out of theatres, standing in doorways and looking out of windows are practically all Negroes; and then he emerges where the population as suddenly becomes white again. There is nothing just like it in any other city in the country, for there is no preparation for it; no change in the character of the houses and streets; no change, indeed, in the appearance of the people, except their color.

. . . . .

I am informed . . . that the total value of property in Harlem owned and controlled by colored people would at a conservative estimate amount to more than sixty million dollars. These figures are amazing, especially when we take into account the short time in which they have been piled up. Twenty years ago Negroes were begging for the privilege of renting a flat in Harlem. Fifteen years ago barely a half dozen colored men owned real property in all Manhattan. And down to ten years ago the amount that had been acquired in Harlem was comparatively negligible. Today Negro Harlem is practically owned by Negroes.

The question naturally arises, "Are the Negroes going to be able to hold Harlem?" If they have been steadily driven northward for the past hundred years and out of less desirable sections, can they hold this choice bit of Manhattan Island? It is hardly probable that Negroes will hold Harlem indefinitely, but when they are forced out it will not be for the same reasons that forced them out of former quarters in New York City. The situation is entirely different and without precedent. When colored people do leave Harlem, their homes, their churches, their investments and their businesses, it will be because the land has become so valuable they can no longer afford to live on it. But the date of another move northward is very far in the future. What will Harlem be and become in the meantime? Is there danger that the Negro may lose his economic status in New York and be unable to hold his property? Will Harlem become merely a famous ghetto, or will it be a center of intellectual, cultural and economic forces exerting an influence throughout the world, especially upon Negro peoples? Will it become a point of friction between the races in New York?

I think there is less danger to the Negroes of New York of losing out economically and industrially than to the Negroes of any large city in the North. In most of the big industrial centers Negroes are engaged in gang labor. They are employed by thousands in the stock yards in Chicago, by thousands in the automobile plants in Detroit; and in those cities they are likely to be the first to be let go, and in thousands, with every business depression. In New York there is hardly such a thing as gang labor among Negroes, except among the longshoremen, and it is in the longshoremen's unions, above all others, that Negroes stand on an equal footing. Employment among Negroes in New York is highly diversified; in the main they are employed more as individuals than as non-integral parts of a gang. Furthermore, Harlem is gradually becoming more and more a self-supporting community. Negroes there are steadily branching out into new businesses and enterprises in which Negroes are employed. So the danger of great numbers of Negroes being thrown out of work at once, with a resulting economic crisis among them, is less in New York than in most of the large cities of the North to which Southern migrants have come.

These facts have an effect which goes beyond the economic and industrial situation. They have a direct bearing on the future character of Harlem and on the question as to whether Harlem will be a point of friction between the races in New York. It is true that Harlem is a Negro community, well defined and stable; anchored to its fixed homes, churches, institutions, business and amusement places; having its own working, business and professional classes. It is experiencing a constant growth of group consciousness and community feeling. Harlem is therefore, in many respects, typically Negro. It has many unique characteristics. It has movement, color, gaiety, singing, dancing, boisterous laughter and loud talk. One of its outstanding features is brass band parades. Hardly a Sunday passes but that there are several of these parades of which many are gorgeous with regalia and insignia. Almost any excuse will do—the death of an humble member of the Elks, the laying of a corner stone, the "turning out" of the order of this or that. In many of these characteristics it is similar to the Italian colony. But withal, Harlem grows more metropolitan and more a part of New York all the while. Why is it then that its tendency is not to become a mere "quarter"?

I shall give three reasons that seem to me to be important in their order. First, the language of Harlem is not alien; it is not Italian or Yiddish; it is English. Harlem talks American, reads American, thinks American. Second, Harlem is not physically a "quarter." It is not a section cut off. It is merely a zone through which four main arteries of the city run. Third, the fact that there is little or no gang labor gives Harlem Negroes the opportunity for individual expansion and individual contacts with the life and spirit of New York. A thousand Negroes from Mississippi put to work as a gang in a Pittsburgh steel mill will for a long time remain a thousand Negroes from Mississippi. Under the conditions that prevail in New York they would all within six months become New Yorkers. The rapidity with which Negroes become good New Yorkers is one of the marvels to observers.

These three reasons form a single reason why there is small probability that Harlem will ever be a point of race friction between the races in New York. One of the principal factors in the race riot in Chicago in 1919 was the fact that at that time there were 12,000 Negroes employed in gangs in the stock yards.

There was considerable race feeling in Harlem at the time of the hegira of white residents due to the "invasion," but that feeling, of course, is no more. Indeed, a number of the old white residents who didn't go or could not get away before the housing shortage struck New York are now living peacefully side by side with colored residents. In fact, in some cases white and colored tenants occupy apartments in the same house. Many white merchants still do business in thickest Harlem. On the whole, I know of no place in the country where the feeling between the races is so cordial and at the same time so matter-of-fact and taken for granted. One of the surest safeguards against an outbreak in New York such as took place in so many Northern cities in the summer of 1919 is the large proportion of Negro police on duty in Harlem.

To my mind, Harlem is more than a Negro community; it is a large scale laboratory experiment in the race problem. The statement has often been made that if Negroes were transported to the North in large numbers the race problem with all of its acuteness and with new aspects would be transferred with them. Well, 175,000 Negroes live closely together in Harlem, in the heart of New York, 75,000 more than live in any Southern city, and do so without any race friction. Nor is there any unusual record of crime. I once heard a captain of the 38th Police Precinct (the Harlem precinct) say that on the whole it was the most law-abiding precinct in the city. New York guarantees its Negro citizens the fundamental rights of American citizenship and protects them in the exercise of those rights. In return the Negro loves New York and is proud of it, and contributes in his way to its greatness. He still meets with discriminations, but possessing the basic rights, he knows that these discriminations will be abolished.

I believe that the Negro's advantages and opportunities are greater in Harlem than in any other place in the country, and that Harlem will become the intellectual, the cultural and the financial center for Negroes of the United States, and will exert a vital influence upon all Negro peoples.

14 / CINCINNATI OPTS FOR REFORM

Long known for the corruption and misgovernment of its Republican machine, Cincinnati finally broke with its past in a historic election in 1924. This reform, unlike many others, was effective, and the Ohio city remains to this day one of the best administered and progressive municipalities in the country. Henry Bentley, a Cincinnati lawyer and one of the leaders in the successful campaign, describes the strategy and tactics of the reformers.

On November 4, 1924, the people of Cincinnati, by a vote of 92,510 for, 41,105 against, adopted an amendment to the Municipal charter, providing for a council of nine, elected at large by proportional representation and a city Manager, to be selected by such council. The adoption of this amendment was opposed by the local Republican party. Although in the same election the entire Republican county ticket was elected and President Coolidge received in the city of Cincinnati a vote of 92,491, the charter carried by a vote slightly larger than the vote received by President Coolidge. How it happened that the local Republican organization secured fewer than half as many votes against the charter as it polled for its presidential candidate, is the question that is asked again and again, sometimes by mere citizens and other times by the old line machine politicians. The result seems to puzzle both amateurs and professionals.

Of course, a reversal of political advice as gigantic as this would naturally arouse comment in any city. However, when it occurred in a city noted throughout the country for its peculiarly

SOURCE: Henry Bentley, "Why Cincinnati Voted for P. R. and a City Manager," *National Municipal Review,* XIV (February, 1925), 69–74. Reprinted by permission.

powerful political machine, the interest is greatly increased. The editor of the *National Municipal Review* has asked me, as the chairman of the campaign committee in charge of the Cincinnati charter amendment, to express my opinion as to the reasons for so overwhelming a victory.

The prime reason for the victory was the fact that political conditions had become intolerable in Cincinnati and the charter amendment offered a way out. Like all simple explanations, however, this does not explain. For many years there has been dissatisfaction but the political machine has been so strongly intrenched that it has disregarded the discontent. Its task was made easier by certain peculiarities of the old charter of Cincinnati.

No Independent Candidates Possible

The old city charter provided for the federal plan of government. It was unique in two respects. Cincinnati was the only city in the United States of America where a candidate for office could be nominated only at the primaries of a political party. No one could be nominated by petition, and no one could run as an independent. In consequence, since the Democratic party was very weak in Cincinnati, a nomination by the Republican party was equivalent to an election, and little regard was paid to the wishes of the public. Candidates were trained to feel that they were representatives not of the public, but of the party. A peculiar form of party responsibility was thus created. The party executives discussed details of administration and directed the elected officials to do or not to do certain things. The elected officials accepted the recommendation of the party executives and were content to substitute for personal responsibility, this so-called party responsibility.

The other unique feature of the charter was the form of ballot. Twenty-seven cities in Ohio had adopted charters under the home rule provision of the Ohio constitution. Twenty-six of these eliminated the use of party emblems in municipal elections. Cincinnati was the one exception among the charter cities of Ohio. It retained the eagle and the rooster in municipal elections and this made it much easier for the organization in control to poll the ignorant vote.

. . . . .

Before any movement for reform could be started, it was necessary that the public be educated to the defects of the present system. This education was begun by a little organization called the Cincinnatus Association. It was organized by a small number of men, mainly ex-service men, who upon their return from the army were desirous of carrying back into civil life some of the idealism of war service. This organization began an investigation of certain specific phases of city government. For several years it held its meetings twice a month and listened to reports of special committees on specific phases of city administration. Since these discussions were non-political, the newspapers gave them a great deal of publicity. Gradually the public began to be interested in these debates, and at the same time the members began to appreciate that behind the isolated mistakes of administration was a unified force working for inefficient government.

Out of the discussions in this organization was developed the fact that the city was being discriminated against in the division of taxes for the benefit of the county, and that the county was wasting money while the city was maintained upon starvation rations. As a result the special tax levy asked by the city officials was defeated at the polls in 1923. As the result of another paper read at the Cincinnatus Association, a movement was started to abolish the party emblem in municipal elections, and petitions were circulated by the Birdless Ballot League. This movement . . . developed by combination with another group, into a movement for a thorough-going reform, the amendment of the city charter to provide for:

(a) The elimination of the party emblem in municipal elections.

(b) The nomination of candidates by petition only.

(c) The reduction of council from thirty-two to nine, and the election at large instead of by wards.

(d) The use of proportional representation.

(e) The city manager form of government.

. . . . .

Little Money Spent

The minimum expense of a campaign was estimated at $5,000. A small group of interested citizens agreed to contribute whatever sum would prove necessary to bring the popular subscription up to $5,000. This enabled the work to start at once and also permitted the finance committee to wait until public enthusiasm was stirred before soliciting funds. The finance committee, subsequently under the chairmanship of Ralph Holterhoff, established the remarkable record of raising nearly $10,000 and of having a balance of nearly $1,000 in the treasury after settling all expenses of the campaign.

The first steps taken were building a women's organization. Miss Emily R. Kneubuhl was employed as educational director, and Miss Bessie Fennell as business manager. Through the wonderful assistance of the League of Women Voters and the Woman's City Club, an organization of women was perfected in twenty of the twenty-six wards in Cincinnati. Twenty ward chairmen were selected and 465 precinct workers were enlisted under them.

A speakers' bureau was organized and forty-three speakers addressed over three hundred meetings. . . .

At each meeting addressed, cards were passed among the audience for signatures volunteering services in some capacity in the fight. In this way, seventy-five volunteers who worked during the campaign in the office, eleven persons who loaned their automobiles for service, 283 witnesses to the count on election day, and many of the 465 precinct workers were secured.

. . . . .

The Charter Committee was aided by a number of fortuitous circumstances that irritated different groups of citizens. The citizens who depended upon street cars for transportation were dissatisfied because the fare had been raised in a few years from five cents to ten cents and was still going up. The citizens who drove automobiles were angry because of the condition of the streets and particularly because it was brought out during the campaign that the city officials had diverted the automobile license fees from the repair of streets, as required by law, to other purposes. The Chamber of Commerce was incensed because [the] council had disregarded the recommendation of an expert employed by it to investigate the gas rate, and over its protest had passed an ordinance increasing the gas rate beyond all reason. Labor was angry because of a suspicion that the candidates nominated for the state legislature by the Committee on Progressive Political Action were counted out in the Republican primaries in August. Certainly there were grounds for this suspicion when the vote in the precincts where labor had witnesses was compared with the vote in precincts where there were no labor witnesses. The charter amendment abolished the precinct count and required a count in daylight at a central counting place. This provision appealed strongly to the men who were resentful against errors in precinct counting.

All of these fortuitous circumstances were seized upon by the Charter Committee, and the appeal for a small council, business management, and honest elections united the citizens as they had never been united before. The result was a victory so overwhelming that even the proponents of the charter can as yet scarcely realize it.

15 / CIVIC SPIRIT

The most widely read survey of an American city is probably the Lynds' study in the 1920's of Muncie, Indiana, a smallish industrial city in the Midwest. Of all the groupings that influenced "Middletown," the Lynds found that it was indeed the business element, already satirized in celebrated novels, that set the tone for twentieth-century urban life.

. . . "Civic loyalty" to "Magic Middletown" is better organized and almost as conspicuous today as in the flamboyant gas boom days when every issue of the press breathed forth boastings and slurs on rival cities. Following a mistaken rumor in 1890 that some of Middletown's ball players were to be given a trip to Europe "to exhibit America's national sport," the press seized the opportunity to exult: "This will be quite a nice trip for the boys and a bigger advertisement than —— can scare up for their dried-up town. [Middletown] is always ahead." "Boom breezes," "natural gas," "the new electric street railway," "50,000 population in ten years," have simply given way to "Shop in Middletown," "Middletown offers more," "Beat 'em Bearcats," "I'm for Middletown College," as focal points of enthusiasm. The European War, like the earlier gas boom, served as the emergency evoking much of this civic loyalty.

"Some time ago," commented a member of Rotary, "one of the papers asked a lot of us what was the most important change we noted in Middletown. I said it was the change in community spirit. In 1910 nobody would help anybody else. Such a thing as the Presidents' Club over here at the Chamber of Commerce that brings the heads of all the civic clubs together would have been out of the question then—the men just wouldn't have come together. The war did it—forcing men to learn to coöperate."

Two activities promoting civic loyalty deserve special mention. The Chamber of Commerce, the successor of the old Citizens' Enterprise Association, while still opposed by many workers as a capitalistic organization, is becoming increasingly a community center. In 1890 the diminutive predecessor of the Chamber of Commerce existed solely to boost business, but in one month in 1924, 157 different meetings sponsored by forty-one different organizations were held in the Chamber of Commerce building. The spirit of the Chamber of Commerce is expressed by a recent president of the organization, "Merchants and farmers, Catholics and Protestants, bankers and working men—we're all living here together, and as far as I can see we're going to have to keep on, and I'm against anything that splits us up against each other."

An even more widespread agency of group cohesion is the high school basket-ball team. In 1890, with no school athletics, such a thing as an annual state high school basket-ball tournament was undreamed of. Middletown claimed, to be sure, a "world's championship" in polo, but the gate receipts reported at the games were small, and the young baker who took in everything about town reports going to only one polo game in three and one-half winter months and then only because a "date" failed him; baseball received much newspaper space, but support for the teams had to be urged. Today more civic loyalty centers around basket-ball than around any other one thing. No distinctions divide the crowds which pack the school gymnasium for home games and which in every kind of machine crowd the roads for out-of-town games. North Side and South Side, Catholic and Kluxer, banker and machinist—their one shout is "Eat 'em, beat 'em, Bearcats!"

. . . . .

At least two values seem patently involved in these various massed boostings of "Magic Middletown" that crop up recurrently in the Chamber of Commerce, in basket-ball, at noonday luncheon clubs, in the suppression of news judged unfavorable, in the desire which one hears expressed over and over that "Middletown make a good showing." One is assurance in the face of the baffling too-bigness of European wars, death, North Poles, ill health, business worries, and political graft; the bigness of it all shrinks at a championship basket-ball game or a Chamber of Commerce rally, and the whole business of living in Middletown suddenly "fits" again, and one "belongs"; one is a citizen of no mean city, and presumably, no mean citizen. This glorification of the homely necessities of living is apparent in the exhortation of an outstanding Middletown club woman to a group of children:

"You must have community spirit. You must think that there is no finer town in the whole United States than this. There is no finer school than yours, no finer parents than yours, no finer opportunities anywhere than you have right here. People talk of California where there is sunshine all the year round, but I've lived in California, and give me Middle Western rains! I tell you there's no lovelier place on God's footstool than this old state of ours."

The other purpose served by civic boosting is the more tangible one of bolstering the crucial getting-a-living activity by which the city lives and prospers. As the local slogan tersely expresses it:

> "United we stick, divided we're stuck.
> United we boost, divided we bust."

"What will become of the town if we don't believe in the thing we're going to manufacture here?" Sherwood Anderson has the citizens of Bidwell ask. "Of course we like Middletown—we have our living here," said a worker's wife. When in the early nineties the paper denounced "the traitors among us who say that gas is failing," the venom in the denunciation came from concern over what such a traitorous occurrence would mean for business. When in 1925 citizens wore cards announcing, "I'm for Middletown College!" it did not mean essentially pride in the college as an educational institution, but, as press and merchants proclaimed, "A live college here will mean thousands of dollars annually for local business." Twenty-five years ago a local editor complained: "We all know how thousands of dollars that should be spent at home are spent in other places by Sunday excursionists. Let us find the remedy!" And today the press still urges, "Shop in Middletown. It should be a matter of civic pride with every citizen to spend his money in the home community." And yet, once thus frankly made instrumental to other things, it is not surprising to observe civic pride openly made secondary to the business interests of this or that group—even of the Chamber of Commerce. When the Chamber remodeled its buildings after a fire it let the contract to the cheapest bidder, a firm which buys none of its mill-work in Middletown, i.e., does not "shop in Middletown"; a local dealer protested at this unpatriotic act, and the secretary of the Chamber hotly rejoined by calling him "uncivic" and a "knocker." Speaking of the smoke nuisance, one of the city's civic liabilities, a member of Rotary said, "The trouble is a lot of our prominent men own stock in the Electric Light Company down here that is one of the worst smoke offenders, and if we tried to do something about it over at the Chamber of Commerce they'd blow cold air on it and kill the scheme. Why, look at these grade crossings, too; our traffic is held up sometimes as much as forty-five minutes right down here on the main street, and that sort of thing hurts business. We got a movement started to elevate the tracks, and then some of the manufacturers learned it would inconvenience them in loading their cars and they killed it. . . ."

. . . . .

The foregoing pages have suggested various factors tending to decrease and to increase the cohesion of the community. A final point remains to be suggested. It was noted in an earlier chapter that the working class, particularly the males, appear to be more isolated as members of the group than formerly. In the present chapter indications have been strong that the cohesion and conformity of the business class is proceeding very rapidly. In other words, the sense of "belonging," of fitting their world—none the less real psychologically though possibly based on nothing more substantial than symbols—appears to be growing more rapidly among the business class than among the workers. The one group gives more easily with the stresses to which the group is subject, because its members have built their lives about these dominant stresses at more points; it does the "civic" thing easily, because civic values are its values at so many points. The workers, on the other hand, instead of yielding to and reinforcing the pressures of this organized community life, are more often inert, uncoöperative, and even resistant, as in the case of their opposition to the Chamber of Commerce; the major drives of "Magic Middletown" are not so completely their drives, and only at second hand do they tingle to the exhilaration of some of the things that are living itself to the business group.

16 / DINOSAUR CITIES

A widely-known designer of garden cities, Clarence S. Stein, describes the evils of urban congestion and uncontrolled growth.

Most of us see the Great City as in a dream. It is the sum of all our possible aspirations. A picturesque skyline, massive towers, romantic beauty! Crowds swaying through the lighted streets in pursuit of pleasure; flashing lights, dancing feet, and delightful foods with the flavor of Rome, Paris, Vienna, Peking or London. A far cry from the Ladies' Social of Gopher Prairie! Libraries

SOURCE: Clarence S. Stein, "Dinosaur Cities," *The Survey: Graphic Number*, LIV (May 1, 1925), 134–38.

of rare books, vast museums and universities, the grand opera and the concert hall—the city of culture!

Our dream does not stop here; it has also a practical side. We see successful lawyers, engineers, advertising men, seated behind wide mahogany desks, protected and padded by secretaries, or speeding out to the golf-links and the country estate—the city of great opportunities! Chicago and New York, or at least Philadelphia, Boston, St. Louis and Los Angeles, lie at the end of that long, long trail which winds into the land of our dreams. Even if we remain in the home town, our aim is to make it grow fast enough to put us in the same class as these cities.

It is cruel to put the hard realities of daylight alongside these dream cities. But sooner or later most of us in the great cities awake to find that we have been grasping after a bubble, and that many of the real opportunities of living have slipped through our hands. For the city of our dreams is lost in another city which could occur to a sane mind only in a nightmare. It is in this second city that the great mass of people who swell the census statistics live and work and marry and die.

Look at the great city in its entirety: the turbid mass of traffic blocking the streets and avenues, the slow-moving crowd of people clambering into street-cars, elevateds, subways, their arms pinioned to their sides, pushed and packed like cattle in ill-smelling cars, with a mingling of bodies which would be indecent were it not for the suffocation and discomfort that acts, as it were, as a counterirritant. Look at the dingy slums of the East Side, Long Island City, the stockyard neighborhoods, the Hump, or where you will: there is little enough to choose between the dark unsanitary tenements of lower Manhattan (some of them among the worst in the world) and the grey minimum of decency that West Philadelphia provides. What part does art, literature, culture, or financial opportunity play in the lives of the millions of men and women who go through the daily routine of life in our great urban districts? The city of dreams is as far away from them as it is from the denizen of Winesburg, Ohio.

To the few the great city gives all: to the millions it gives annually less and less. In spite of sanitary codes, tenement house laws, and various other urban reforms, the prospects for decent human living have become distinctly worse in New York during the last generation. And New York, unfortunately, represents the goal towards which all our bigger centers are striving with might and main. For this reason I propose to examine New York's plight in greater detail, and to ask: Why the Great City? What are we putting into the Great City, and what are we getting out of it? How long can we stand the strains and difficulties that are peculiar to our large congested centers? What particular promise is there in planning for an increasing population in other large centers, if all these efforts are doomed eventually to result in the same difficulties? Is the Great City still the goal of our legitimate desires, or is it a monstrosity, a bloated spider that lures us into its web only to devour us?

. . . . .

Congestion is such a normal process in the great city, and decent living quarters require such a restriction on the profits of the speculative builder, that even on the edge of the city, where the price of land remains comparatively low, four and five story tenements are erected. Superficial observers talk of this housing breakdown as if it were a product of the war. On the contrary, there is a chronic deficiency that has been piling up in every great city—in London, Paris, and Berlin, as well as in American cities—for the last hundred years. In the great city there are not enough decent quarters to go round; and even the decent quarters are not good enough. That is the sum and substance of the housing breakdown. In the acutest stages of the housing crisis the smaller centers in New York state did not feel the shortage as keenly as the great city. One can almost put the case in a mathematical form: the bigger the city the remoter are its chances of solving the housing problem. This does not, of course, ignore the fact that other causes than congestion have created housing difficulties quite frequently in small cities, and even villages.

. . . . .

. . . The great city can avoid a complete breakdown only by building an elaborate plant and equipment which enables it temporarily to meet the problem. But it does this with blind disregard for expense. The growth of the city might be illimitable if its purse were illimitable; since the ingenuities of engineering can solve many of our difficulties if we can disregard the expense. The point is that the expense is becoming unbearable. The "overhead" of the city is increasing to a point at which it will outmeasure any of its tangible or intangible benefits. Then something must happen: something which will not be more growth and more expense.

We come now to the breakdown of the street system, and the inability of our overground and underground ways to carry the load of traffic. Our older cities were planned for four-story buildings at most. With the rise of the six-story building in the middle of the last century, traffic difficulties were felt in the shopping district of lower Broadway. An experimental safety bridge was even built. Today, not only in the lower part of Manhattan, but in vast sections between the Pennsylvania and the Grand Central Railroad stations, up Park Avenue and Broadway, and even over in Brooklyn—*today from two to six cities* have been piled up one above the other. This would be bad enough if only foot traffic and public vehicles were considered: the automobile has added the proverbial last straw, for each car, with its two or three occupants, occupies at least twice, and sometimes three or four times the space of pedestrians walking. Since our zoning in the built-up parts of the city has all been done in subservience to rising land values, none of our zoning provisions touch this problem; on the contrary, even in parts of the city where the four-story town has lingered, the twenty-story town is permitted —in fact, is being built. If our avenues were wide enough to carry comfortably the present and potential load of traffic, there would not, in a great many parts of the city, be room for the buildings themselves.

Our city officials and engineers are now hinting that the "solution" lies in building overhead streets. But even if it were conceivable that a complete system of aerial streets could be built for the population, this could be done *only at a cost which would fall back upon the land in the shape of taxes—and in turn this would make it necessary to build higher buildings and more streets!* To call this circle vicious scarcely does it justice. In point of fact no large city, however unbalanced its budget, attempts to keep up with its need for free channels of circulation. Every day the congestion increases—in spite of traffic policemen, curb setbacks, one-way streets, electric traffic signals. Even in Los Angeles, whose growth was coincident with the auto, the cars have multiplied faster than the streets have been widened. The end here is already in sight. There must come a time when every street in New York will be regulated as the streets in the financial district now are: individual vehicles will not be permitted to circulate through the business and industrial sections during the day. This is what happened in prosperous commercial Rome when its congestion reached something like New York's present pitch; and it is inevitable here. It is equally inevitable in Pittsburgh's triangle, where it is now actively discussed, and in Chicago's Loop. And all the while the costs are piling up. The hard, practical men who think they can avoid this conclusion while they continue to congest the population and raise the land values are living in dreamland: they simply have not the courage to face the results of their own handiwork.

The breakdown of the mechanical means of transportation follows hard upon the collapse of the street system; the same causes are at work. As the city increases in height it increases also in area; for the railroad and subway must be introduced to carry the main load of passengers from the central district of skyscraper offices and lofts to the outlying areas. When the vacant land on the outskirts is filled up, the net result is congestion at both ends. This causes a demand for additional means of transportation. Beyond a point which big cities reach at a very early point in their career, more transportation routes mean more congestion. The only way this could be avoided is by duplicating the existing transportation lines; but this method would reduce the earnings of the existing lines by distributing the load, and it is never even considered except when an equal degree of congestion can be assured to the new line. The cost of all these facilities increases steadily as the lines are lengthened into more remote areas so that in one way or another a subsidy must be introduced to support them at a price per ride the ordinary commuter can afford.

. . . . .

As things go now, on the other hand, there is no way in any of the large centers of avoiding a continuous breakdown in its transit facilities. They are, and they must remain, perpetually inadequate so long as people and industries, instead of being redistributed into planned communities, are sucked blindly into the metropolitan areas.

. . . . .

. . . I have used New York merely for the sake of concrete example. New York's problem of housing in 1850 was Chicago's problem in 1890; New York's transit solution of 1900 is now Chicago's solution of 1925—and promises no better; and so on with the other details in the breakdown. Other cities can avoid New York's breakdown only by making an effort to avoid New York's "greatness."

Now all these breakdowns are costly in themselves; unfortunately the effort to put them off becomes even more costly. The result is that money and effort which should go into making the city more liveable—the money that should be spent on the education of children, on the maintenance of health, upon art, education, and culture—all this money and effort is devoted to expenditures which do no more than make the physical side of congestion barely tolerable. It is not merely that the effort to supply sufficient transportation routes, to widen streets sufficiently, is inevitably doomed to failure: what is worse is that even if it were successful it would be foolish and extravagant.

. . . . .

We must do all that is necessary to combat the forces of congestion at their source. For in that direction lie the fundamental things that men and women care most deeply for—a beautiful environment, a home for children, an opportunity to enjoy the day's leisure and the ability to ride on the Juggernaut of industry, instead of being prostrated under its wheels.

17 / REGIONAL PLANNING

The most celebrated of American critics of the modern city, Lewis Mumford sees "regional planning" as the only way out of the headlong race to the "dinosaur city" described in the previous selection.

The hope of the city lies outside itself. Focus your attention on the cities—in which more than half of us live—and the future is dismal. But lay aside the magnifying glass which reveals, for example, the hopelessness of Broadway and Forty-second Street, take up a reducing glass and look at the entire region in which New York lies. The city falls into focus. Forests in the hill-counties, water-power in the mid-state valleys, farmland in Connecticut, cranberry bogs in New Jersey, enter the picture. To think of all these acres as merely tributary to New York, to trace and strengthen the lines of the web in which the spider-city sits unchallenged, is again to miss the clue. But to think of the region as a whole and the city merely as one of its parts—that may hold promise.

Not merely a wistful hope of a better environment, but sheer necessity, leads us thus to change our approach to the problem. For cities . . . are becoming too big; as they grow they fall behind in the barest decencies of housing; they become more expensive to operate, more difficult to police, more burdensome to work in, and more impossible to escape from even in the hours of leisure that we achieve. The forces that have created the great cities make permanent improvement within them hopeless; our efforts to plan them lag pitifully behind the need when indeed

SOURCE: Lewis Mumford, "Regions—To Live In," *The Survey: Graphic Number,* LIV (May 1, 1925), 151–52.

they do not foster the very growth that is becoming insupportable. . . .

. . . Regional planning asks not how wide an area can be brought under the aegis of the metropolis, but how the population and civic facilities can be distributed so as to promote and stimulate a vivid, creative life throughout a whole region—a region being any geographic area that possesses a certain unity of climate, soil, vegetation, industry and culture. The regionalist attempts to plan such an area so that all its sites and resources, from forest to city, from highland to water level, may be soundly developed, and so that the population will be distributed so as to utilize, rather than to nullify or destroy, its natural advantages. It sees people, industry and the land as a single unit. Instead of trying, by one desperate dodge or another, to make life a little more tolerable in the congested centers, it attempts to determine what sort of equipment will be needed for the new centers. It does not aim at urbanizing automatically the whole available countryside; it aims equally at ruralizing the stony wastes of our cities. . . . The civic objective of the regional planning movement is summed up with peculiar accuracy in the concept of the garden-city.

There are a hundred approaches to regional planning; it brings to a head, in fact, a number of movements and methods which have been gathering momentum during the last twenty or thirty years. But each approach has this in common with the others; it attempts to promote a fuller kind of life, at every point in the region. No form of industry and no type of city are tolerable that take the joy out of life. Communities in which courtship is furtive, in which babies are an unwelcome handicap, in which education, lacking the touch of nature and of real occupations, hardens into a blank routine, in which people achieve adventure only on wheels and happiness only by having their minds "taken off" their daily lives—communities like these do not sufficiently justify our modern advances in science and invention.

. . . The community planning movement in America, and the garden-cities movement in England are definite attempts to build up a more exhilarating kind of environment—not as a temporary haven of refuge but as a permanent seat of life and culture, urban in its advantages, permanently rural in its situation. This movement toward garden cities is a movement towards a higher type of civilization than that which has created our present congested centers. It involves a change in aim as well as a change of place. Our present congested districts are the results of the crude applications of the mechanical and mathematical sciences to social development; our garden cities represent fuller development of the more humane arts and sciences—biology and medicine and psychiatry and education and architecture. As modern engineering has made Chicago or New York physically superior to Athens, whilst the labyrinth of subways and high buildings is more deficient for complete living than a Stone Age cave, so we may expect that the cities of tomorrow will not merely embody all that is good in our modern mechanical developments, but also all that was left out in this one-sided existence, all the things that fifth century Athens or thirteenth century Florence, for all their physical crudity, possessed.

On its economic side, this movement towards a fuller human environment goes hand in hand with what has been aptly called the industrial counterrevolution. For a hundred years in America business has been concentrating financial resources, concentrating factories and urban districts, attempting to create material prosperity by producing goods which could be quickly "turned over." The paper values have increased enormously even in the brief period from 1900 to 1920; but most statisticians seem agreed that the real wages of the majority of workers have remained nearly stationary. The new industrial revolution is an attempt to spread the real income of industry by decentralizing industry, by removing some of the burden of the business overhead and sales-promotion, ground rents in congested districts, and so forth. . . . Regional planning is an attempt to turn industrial decentralization—the effort to make the industrial mechanism work better—to permanent social uses. It is an attempt to realize the gains of modern industry in permanent houses, gardens, parks, playgrounds and community institutions.

Finally, regional planning is the New Conservation—the conservation of human values hand in hand with natural resources. Regional planning sees that the depopulated countryside and the congested city are intimately related; it sees that we waste vast quantities of time and energy by ignoring the potential resources of a region, that is, by forgetting all that lies between the terminal points and junctions of our great railroads. Permanent agriculture instead of land-skinning, permanent forestry instead of timber mining, permanent human communities, dedicated to life, liberty and the pursuit of happiness, instead of camps and squatter-settlements, and to stable building, instead of the scantling and falsework of our "go-ahead" communities—all this is embodied in regional planning.

. . . . .

Moreover the aim of regional planning is not confined to those who are interested in the development of industries and resources. The cultural forces that have begun to challenge the dominance of the big city are plainly working in the same direction. So the little theater movement, by building local centers of culture instead of waiting patiently for the crumbs dropped from our metropolitan table, is essential to regionalism; and in the same way our new experimental schools, which have showed the rich educational opportunities that come from exploring and utilizing the whole living environment rather than sticking to the pallid routine of books, find themselves handicapped in the existing centers and demand a new environment patterned on the human scale, in which the school may work intimately in touch with the home and with industry and with the surrounding world of nature.

In sum, regional planning does not mean the planning of big cities beyond their present areas; it means the reinvigoration and rehabilitation of whole regions so that the products of culture and civilization, instead of being confined to a prosperous minority in the congested centers, shall be available to everyone at every point in a region where the physical basis for a cultivated life can be laid down. The technical means of achieving this new distribution of power and culture are at hand. The question before us is whether the automatic operation of physical and financial forces is to burke our rising demand for a more vital and happy kind of existence, or whether, by coordinating our efforts and imaginatively grasping our opportunity, we can remold our institutions so as to promote a regional development—development that will eliminate our enormous economic wastes, give a new life to stable agriculture, set down fresh communities planned on a human scale, and, above all, restore a little happiness and freedom in places where these things have been pretty well wrung out. . . . Will man in America learn the art of mastering and ordering his environment, to promote his own fuller purposes, or will he be mastered by his environment, and presently, as in Samuel Butler's picture in Erewhon, or in Zamiatin's We, find himself without any purposes other than those of the Machine?

18 / RECREATION IN THE CITY

In this study, made at the request of the Council of Social Agencies of Rochester, the Little Theater Movement and the dance-hall problem in a middle-sized industrial city are examined. To conduct the study the Council employed Charles B. Raitt, former superintendent of playgrounds in Los Angeles and participant in a national survey of parks and playgrounds.

Rochester's Community Theater

. . . . .

Founded in 1924, by perseverance and hard work, this community theater has grown from a floundering, homeless infant into a well organized and successful institution, and by its many successes has earned a prominent place in the amateur theatrical world.

SOURCE: Charles B. Raitt, *A Survey of Recreational Facilities in Rochester, N.Y.* (Rochester: Joseph M. Egloff, Printer, 1929), pp. 326–30.

The course followed by the local group in attaining its present prestige is a repetition of that of other similar groups. Community theaters or little theaters as they sometimes are called, now are operating in many cities scattered over the United States. Each successful venture of this type is of interest as it encourages and shows the way for others to follow.

The Community Theater organization is a supporting body or group of persons, interested primarily in amateur players, membership in which is granted on payment of a ten dollar seasonal fee. This fee entitles the member to two tickets for each of six regular presentations given during the season. Thus each member not only is well repaid for the investment, but is lending support to a worthwhile project, a project which is entitled to every possible assistance from the citizens of Rochester.

The Community Players themselves generally are amateur actors of more or less ability and are selected and coached for their particular parts by a professional, trained director. While most of the players are participating for the mere joy and pleasure of it, and also for the opportunity afforded for giving wholesome entertainment to others, by actual experience, this, to several of the local actors, has been a stepping stone to higher and better positions in the field of dramatic art.

A very important and essential factor in this movement is the theater structure itself. The various experiences of community players in finding and acquiring a permanent home usually unfolds an interesting story, generally one of struggle and perseverance. This struggle to acquire a home is part of the big game which makes the ultimate accomplishment worthwhile. After all, as in most undertakings, the things worthwhile and which are appreciated, are those that come after effort and struggle.

Rochester's Community Theater is a converted church building which was acquired after several years of "barnstorming" experiences by the players. This structure has been rehabilitated and altered to meet the many requirements necessary in preparing and presenting the various stage productions. The new home is an interesting one, because it is not only a theatrical center, but it is a center where various social and civic functions are held; where the problems of the organization are talked over; where the numerous plays of the past, present and future are discussed; where costumes, scenery and other stage paraphernalia are designed and made, and where the final complete production is presented for entertainment and approval of the ever critical audience. This plain, simple, little theater, with its 500 seating capacity, is truly an interesting place.

Rochester's Community Theater organization has attained its present high standing after many struggles, and no doubt will continue and carry on to higher levels. Its efforts should be given every encouragement and its work deserves the loyal support of every interested citizen in order that it might render a bigger and better service. Such an organization indeed is a credit to Rochester.

Commercial Dance Halls and Dancing in Rochester

The dance problem in Rochester, as in most other cities, continues to be a source of worry to those who are vitally interested in the social and recreational welfare of our youths and young men and women. The chief concern for worry over this question has to do with morals. Morals in a dance hall usually are directly influenced by the environment, character and actions of associates, type of dance, and quality of leadership and supervision. Accordingly, as these conditions are wholesome or not, the resultant influence of the dance will be for good or bad.

Many social and recreational leaders are inclined to take a narrow view of the situation and feel that no good can result from participation in this form of amusement. There are the few rather restricted in their viewpoint who, in order to correct the evil, would eliminate the social dance entirely. On the other hand, there are those of a more practical trend who have studied and analyzed the problem that feel there is much to be said in favor of the social dance. As a form of physical exercise and also as a means of social intercourse, the dance has values which can well be emphasized, particularly where it involves the young folks not yet out of their teens. Like most other forms of amusement, there is opportunity for abuse and, therefore, criticism. Facing the facts, however, it nevertheless is true that we have the dance; there are those who will dance; we have the dance halls; and we continue to have the problem. Therefore, it is essential that some attempt be made to improve conditions which surround our youths in their search for companionship and amusement during their leisure hours.

The establishment of dance halls and the promotion of public dances on a purely commercial basis, where the enforcement of regulations and maintenance of standards is apt to affect the financial profits, without doubt, has much to do with the creation of this dance problem. The regulation and control of dance halls are a matter of general public concern only insofar as they involve the health, the morals and safety of those who attend. In most cities there are regulatory ordinances, charter provisions, or state statutes which regulate and control to some degree the use and management of these halls. Frequently, these legislative enactments, not only are inadequate for proper regulation and control, but make little or no provision for enforcement.

. . . Some authoritative public department or official should be empowered to see that rules and regulations governing behavior and conduct in dance halls are enforced.

Just what public official or department of the city government can best handle this situation has been a point for discussion for many years. Some have contended that insofar as it is a problem involving recreation, it should be relegated to the department of recreation. The consensus of opinion, however, is that best results can be accomplished by delegating the responsibility to a specially created division or bureau of the police department; namely the policewomen's bureau. It is possible to select women ably qualified to handle the dance hall problems and who are particularly interested in the social and recreational welfare of those who patronize these affairs. The need is for intelligence, tact, forcefulness, personality and sympathetic understanding in supervision rather than a severe, critical and negative attitude so frequently taken by policemen.

Control and supervision thru this agency should be exerted over any and all dances where the public, whether in small or large groups, congregates. Dances properly conducted would naturally require little or no supervision, while those operated under lax management necessarily would demand more attention. The proper legislation should be enacted granting this bureau the authority to supervise, where deemed advisable, any dance-hall or dance conducted as a commercial enterprise, in public institutions, in public places, or under private auspices. All dance halls should be licensed and each dance should be allowed only on permit issued from police headquarters.

To properly enforce rules and regulations governing dances, particularly at commercial halls and places where large groups gather, it is essential that at least one inspector or supervisor from the policewomen's bureau be present during the entire period for each dance. This supervision should be maintained regularly at commercial halls and in each instance the cost should be met by the management.

After observation and study of dance halls in Rochester it was found that, while many dances were being properly conducted, frequently there were cases of negligence in enforcement of certain regulations which are essential to the proper conduct of these halls. It is true in most instances on the part of the various managers, there is a willingness to cooperate with the city officials in enforcement of regulations.

The outstanding and more glaring objectionable occurrences which have been observed in some of Rochester's dance halls are:

Allowing persons under age to enter dance halls.
Operating dances with insufficient lighting.
Extreme jazzy orchestra music.
Use of profanity and boisterous talk.
Over-familiarity and improper behavior by boys and girls.
Use of liquor and allowing intoxicated persons in hall.

Cheek to cheek dancing and too close bodily contact by dancing couples; also extreme jerking and wiggly actions by those dancing.

A very serious practice is that which occurs at the entrance of a busy downtown dance hall. At closing time young men and sometimes older ones driving in autos arrive at the entrance and invite the girls for a ride. Also on these occasions some rather impertinent and embarrassing remarks are made to the girls.

The more serious offences have been observed in only two dance halls.

In Rochester, the responsibility for inspection and enforcement of dance hall regulations is in the hands of a policewoman. The service rendered under the present system of inspection is entirely inadequate, due to the fact that one inspector cannot be several places at one time, and also because her mode of travel is mainly by foot or street car. Under such conditions it is possible to merely scratch the surface in supervising the many dances conducted during the fall and winter seasons.

On several visits to dance halls with one of the policewomen it was quite noticeable that there was plenty for her to do. In practically every instance where open dances were operating there was improper dancing, frequently there was poor or dim lighting, and often one or two girls were requested to leave as being under age. Sometimes on our entrance the floormen would immediately speak to couples dancing and again the lights would come on brighter, thus indicating effective results of a visit by the policewoman. This is only an indication of what there is to do and what might be done with adequate supervision and control.

. . . . .

There is opportunity for a bit of constructive work in bettering dance hall conditions in Rochester. With reasonable regulations, able leadership and adequate assistance; and with the cooperation of dance hall managers, which is reasonable to expect, there is every reason to believe that much headway can be made in solving the perplexing dance hall problem. Best of all this would assure the establishment and maintenance of high standards of etiquette and behavior and provide for more wholesome conditions surrounding the dances attended by the youth of this city.

19 / GANGSTER CIVIC CONSCIOUSNESS

In an ironic editorial, The New York Times *comments on Chicago society where gang leaders, like other leading citizens, deplore the fouling of their city's image by parvenus.*

After a season of books and articles about gangsters, the public would have been depressed if it had appeared that the racketeers annoying actors in Chicago are that city's first-grade gunmen. Investigation has revealed that the persons who attempted various hold-ups of Miss Francine Larrimore, Mr. Charles Winninger and Mr. Groucho Marx were small-fry. They tried ignoble devices, such as efforts to sell tickets to imaginary "benefits," accompanied by threats of punishment if the tickets were not bought. A blackmail note, demanding $1,000 was sent to Miss Larrimore. The police, informed of these demonstrations against visiting actors, promptly furnished bodyguards. But Chicago's eminent gang leaders were not satisfied with mere protective action. They expressed formal regret that these trifling demonstrations should have been connected with the real gangs of the city. Mr. Eddie Cantor was welcomed at a Cicero cabaret, where it was made quite pointed that he was a friend of the distinguished proprietor, whose word rules a large section of the population. Another renowned leader suggested that if Miss Larrimore would dine with him in public it would be sufficient notice to the jackals that the lion would stand for no poaching. There have

SOURCE: "Chicago's Fair Name," *The New York Times,* February 28, 1930.

been many demonstrations of hospitality in this country, but few have been so significant.

There is another aspect to the situation. It is civic pride. Having given Chicago a reputation as the situs of organized gang war and machine-gun massacre, the underworld generals were embarrassed by the character and triviality of the moves against actors. What would the country think? To feel was to act, and the result is that the visiting Thespians realize the difference between real A 1 gang leaders and lilliputians in the "racket." It has also been made clear to them that, as Alexander spared the house of Pindar, so the stage—and especially the musical stage—is immune. Gunners must have their relaxation like other mortals; in fact, the tension under which they labor calls for it. They are conserving their own interests when they move to keep actors free from worry. Juliets, ready at any moment to dodge bullets, cannot exert their full talent. The stage and all the artistic elements of the nation will note with appreciation what Chicago's responsible gangsters have done.

PART IV

The City in Depression

THE salient fact about the early 1930's was the Great Depression. Never before had so many persons been visibly affected by an economic collapse. With most Americans now living in places defined as urban by the Bureau of the Census, there was less opportunity than had been available in the past to subsist, at the very least, on food raised on the farm. The cities felt the blow of the Crash almost immediately and suffered from its effects for many years.

Within a year of the stock market collapse of October, 1929, millions of men and women were unemployed, and most rapidly lost hope of finding jobs. Relief agencies were unequipped to deal with mass unemployment and deprivation; desperate improvisation became the order of the day (Selection 20). The situation worsened steadily and by November, 1932, the cities were facing bankruptcy (Selection 21) in their efforts to meet undeniable need. When the unemployed tried to solve their problems in their own way, they were occasionally swayed by Communists who hoped that a revolutionary situation had arrived. More often, the unemployed resorted to selling apples or creating "Hoovervilles" (Selection 22).

With so many persons having only time to spend, the young recreation movement found itself called upon to provide services beyond anything anticipated. Frequently, the undermanned and underpaid staffs responded with ingenuity to this unexpected opportunity to demonstrate their value (Selection 23).

The problems of governing the cities were complicated not only by the requirement of feeding their populations, but by the needlessly complex and archaic systems of overlapping government that existed in most places. Often it was impossible for a concerned citizen to know just where responsibility lay (Selection 24). In Chicago, moreover, multiple government and depression were not the only troubles: crime still flourished, influence ruled, and the best will in the world could not help a police commissioner do his job properly (Selection 25).

20 / THE FIRST YEAR OF DEPRESSION

Gertrude Springer, an associate editor of The Survey, *principal organ of social workers, summarizes the reports from relief administrators, public and private, showing the unprecedented demands for help only one year after the Crash.*

"A thousand men are sleeping nightly on the lower level of Michigan Avenue along a loading platform of one of the big buildings while the automobiles roll by overhead and the winter has not yet begun, though the nights are cold." *Chicago.*

"Fifteen hundred men are sleeping outdoors. They have no work and must find shelters in doorways and corners as best they can." *Pittsburgh.*

"The Sisters at St. Vincent's Hospital give bread and a cup of soup to whoever comes to their door, but the numbers have mounted to hundreds and the Sisters fear that they cannot continue to feed them." *New York.*

SOURCE: Gertrude Springer, "Unemployment: The Burden of Mass Relief," *The Survey,* LXV (November 15, 1930), 199–202.

And the winter is still ahead.

There can be no doubt of the distress signals. They are flying at every turn in every city of the country. The clouds of unemployment show no rifts and the scurrying crowds of victims of the storm grow steadily in numbers and in misery.

All the agencies of relief, strained as they are by months of unremitting pressure, are stripped for action in a situation which conservative observers regard as of disaster proportions. The niceties of modern social work, the careful processes of building and rehabilitation are going overboard. The struggle is reduced to the simple elements of food and shelter for the hungry and the homeless.

The heaviest weight of distress falls on the cities. Added to their own load, inevitable in an industrial depression, is the steady migration from towns and small communities which the most urgent advice and warning is powerless to stem. The setting up of necessary relief machinery, with its unavoidable publicity, brings to a city a new stream of distress pushing its way blindly and unreasoningly toward any gleam of hope. Wide-range planning for relief has its place in the whole picture, but when it comes down to the bare facts of food and shelter, it is the community organization that holds the bag, the community that must measure its problem and muster its resources to deal with it.

Statistics gathered by Ralph Hurlin of the Russell Sage Foundation from the public-relief departments of twenty-two medium-sized cities show that between August 1929 and August 1930 the number of families aided increased 146 per cent. . . . Fourteen public-relief departments that have reported show a rise of 9.7 per cent in aggregate relief in September over August, while thirty-one non-sectarian family societies show a rise of 2.2 per cent. The smaller increase for the private agencies as compared with the public is accounted for by the fact that several large societies in the reporting group were forced by lack of funds to refuse new cases and to reduce drastically the relief expenditures on the old ones.

Private relief agencies everywhere frankly admit their lack of resources to cope alone with such a situation. But fortunately many cities have developed, in the past ten years, a working arrangement between public and private agencies which divides the load logically and minimizes the danger of indiscriminate dumping of responsibility by one on the other. In Boston, for instance, the whole burden of unemployment relief is carried by the Overseers of the Poor. The Family Society supplements Overseers' aid in special cases, and in many instances gives service where the entire financial help comes from public funds. . . . The City Council has just appropriated an additional $1,000,000 for this purpose, and has approved a popular subscription of $2,000,000 for further family relief. It is not clear how this fund will be raised or disbursed.

Milwaukee has much the same situation as Boston. Here a reorganization of the public department occurred coincidentally with the beginning of the unemployment period. Here the department assumes full responsibility for all non-resident cases and all straight unemployment cases hitherto unknown to social agencies.

. . . . .

Unhappily, all the pictures of public and private cooperation in the emergency are not so encouraging. From Toledo, A City the Auto Ran Over, comes another story. Wendell F. Johnson, director of the Social Service Federation, says;

> The situation as reflected in relief demands is getting rapidly worse. The number of families under care is about four times as great as it was a year ago, and relief expenditures are proportionately higher. The heaviest drain is upon city funds. The city is putting up to the voters in November a bond issue for $750,000 which, if passed, will be used as wages for part-time work for men in need of relief. Since this agency handles public funds, we cannot limit our intake. Standards of work are, of course, suffering, since the average case load per worker is mounting to almost impossible heights.

On the whole, the agencies in cities with even a skeleton organization for outdoor relief seem in better condition to cope with the storm than those where the entire burden rests on private machinery. In Cleveland, which has no outdoor system, the agencies see their only hope in a work fund to provide immediate employment for those most needing it. A bond issue of $200,000 for work in the parks is now assured. The Cleveland Community Fund in adopting its budget for next year took cognizance of the plight of the family societies by increasing their allotments by 28 per cent. Since the total budget was held at the 1930 figure of $4,650,000, these increases were only at the expense of other types of work. Neighborhood agencies were cut 22.5 per cent, character-building 12 per cent, health-promotion 14 per cent, and hospitals 6 per cent.

. . . . .

But with all this shifting of funds and with the hope that the bond issue will ease the pressure, Cleveland still faces the inescapable conclusion that at least another half million will be needed to ward off actual want from its people. And so it has tied an emergency tail onto the Community Fund kite—an extra emergency fund of $750,000 to meet the present extraordinary need. Pledges for this will be sought only from the "higher bracket," contributors of $100 or more, and only after the subscriber has equaled his contribution of last year. A third of this special fund is already ear-marked for the deficits which the relief agencies, with disconcerting unanimity, have been rolling up since midsummer.

Philadelphia, which discontinued public outdoor relief in 1879, has been forced by the present stress to return to it. This year $150,000 was appropriated on an emergency basis. This was exhausted in the late summer. Under pressure from the Committee of One Hundred, led by Jacob Billikopf, and the All-Philadelphia Community Council, led by Karl deSchweinitz, an item of $200,000 for family relief has been put into the budget for 1931. "But meantime," says Mr. Billikopf, "families supported by the department with its emergency fund are in dire distress."

The Philadelphia Family Society has had a hard year. Its relief funds enabled it to care for an average of 750 families a month, but that peak was reached in the early spring and no new case could be accepted unless an old one was closed or some benevolent individual made a special contribution. The end of

March the Welfare Federation allotted $20,000 to the Society for emergency relief. Immediately the case load soared to 1059. But in three months this fund was exhausted and the Society was obliged to cut back to its March basis. This static condition will continue until more funds are provided by the Welfare Federation. The Society has asked for an additional $100,000 for relief the coming year.

In St. Louis, which has no municipal system of outdoor relief, the Provident Association . . . found its relief deficit mounting to such heights that it was forced to stop intake and to cut down to bare necessities the service to its two thousand open cases. . . .

. . . . .

Detroit's proud boast that it does all its relief work with public funds without recourse to private charity is put to a severe test by the present situation, for Detroit has been hard hit by the depression and the needs of its people are pressing. Mayor Frank Murphy rode into office on a high wave of promises to find work for the idle. A count showed that one hundred thousand of them were ready to hold him to his promise and that of these some twenty thousand were hungry. There has been so much drum-beating over the Detroit situation that it is not easy to estimate the efficacy of Mayor Murphy's far-flung program. The stress of midwinter will put it to the test. Social workers find much to criticize, yet the fact remains that he has succeeded in organizing the whole city, with little partisan discord, into a united effort to supply immediate jobs and relief, and to swing all resources into a work program calculated to last out the winter. His committees are busily at work staggering industrial shifts, arranging for the conversion of timber on waste land into cordwood, drumming up odd jobs, and consolidating neighborhood chores into full days' work. They are pushing forward such public improvements as are already financed, and urging the financing of new ones. In relief activities, a special committee has raised a fund on which grocery, fuel, and rent orders for families are drawn. The next step will be to set up soup kitchens and lodgings for the homeless. All employment and all relief is rigidly restricted, in theory at least, to persons who have been residents of Detroit for at least a year.

And, finally, New York with its great sprawling problems of unemployment and of relief, problems so overgrown that they yield to no comparisons! The census last April gave New York about 254,000 unemployed. Labor leaders put the figure today at 300,000 for organized labor alone. What the total may be is anyone's guess. New York has had no direct outdoor relief since 1897, the weight of general family care falling on privately supported charities. The city budget for 1931 shows heavy increases in items of relief, but these are for various specific purposes, their distribution determined by statute, and hold little prospect of easing the burden of the private agencies. These, with their expenditures already double those of a year ago, are facing a winter of unprecedented difficulty. Applicants ineligible for any of the city funds are a steadily mounting tide. How high it will rise when winter sets in and seasonal employment suffers its annual slump, no one dares to predict.

. . . . .

. . . Social workers shake their heads, "All we can do is the best we can, get all the money we can, and make it go as far as we can. There will be no frills on social work this winter."

21 / THE COST AFTER THREE YEARS

Two years later the situation for the cities and their populations had become even worse, as Frank Bane of the American Public Welfare Association grimly pointed out. Need had increased greatly and many cities had all but exhausted their financial resources in efforts to provide even a modicum of subsistence.

Many cities have reached or are reaching the limit of their ability to handle the fast mounting relief load that has accumulated during this long continued depression. Private philanthropy and local government together for two long years have struggled with an unemployment problem that is national and even international in its scope. During this last year, several states have made appropriations to aid their political subdivisions in carrying this unprecedented load and now the federal government has come into the picture with a helping hand to states and cities that have done and are continuing to do their utmost. Constitutional limitations, statutory difficulties, and the falling off of revenue from taxation all have hindered the ability of cities and even states to handle this problem.

Statistics compiled by the U.S. Children's Bureau from 125 cities of 50,000 or more population located in all sections of the country make the situation startlingly clear. The total expenditures from 976 agencies and divisions of departments that are giving relief in these cities show an increase for July, 1932, of 87 per cent over July, 1931. This seems more startling when it is remembered that the 1931 annual figures show a 327 per cent increase over 1929. When it is realized that the monthly expendi-

SOURCE: Frank Bane, "Feeding the Hungry," *National Municipal Review*, XXII (November, 1932), 628–33. Reprinted by permission.

tures of these cities, representing one third of the total population of the United States, were $21,760,238 for the month of July, it is easy to understand why the problem of how cities are to finance the greater winter load takes precedence over usual municipal problems.

Cities of varying sizes located in different sections of the country all show the seriousness of this problem. New York, Chicago, Philadelphia and Pittsburgh, Detroit, Los Angeles and San Francisco, Boston, Baltimore, and St. Louis, or cities of smaller size, all tell the same tragic story of increasing relief loads, families with resources completely exhausted and standards of relief declining. . . .

. . . . .

Chicago's Serious Plight

Chicago (Cook County) has come to the end of its resources time after time and has been assisted by the state and recently by the federal government. Conditions were so serious that the Reconstruction Finance Corporation made $3,000,000 available as their first grant on July 27. At that time the Illinois Emergency Relief Commission had only enough funds left from their $18,750,000 fund to last a few days. Soon the $3,000,000 were exhausted and another grant of $6,000,000 was made to carry the state through to the first of October, most of this being made for the Chicago area. Another grant of $5,000,000 was necessary before October 1.

Conditions in Chicago have been steadily growing worse—relief agencies had an additional 8,000 families to care for during the usually quiet month of July. Expenditures for this month were nearly $3,000,000. About 100,000 families (approximately one half million persons) received aid, the average grant amounting to $23.78 per family. In October it was necessary to make a drastic cut in this allowance. Rents are not paid by the relief agencies and housing in certain sections is unspeakably bad. The unemployed number between 600,000 and 700,000 or about 40 per cent of the employable workers with more and more of these being forced to ask for relief. It is estimated that at least $35,000,000 will be spent in 1932 for an inadequate job and that adequate relief would cost at least $50,000,000.

. . . . .

"Starvation" in Philadelphia

The situation in July, 1932, in Philadelphia was described by the Community Council as one of "Slow Starvation and Progressive Disintegration of Family Life." Unemployment has averaged from 40,000 to 50,000 in recent years but by May, 1932, this total had reached 298,000. In June the governor of Pennsylvania estimated that 250,000 persons in Philadelphia "faced actual starvation." Food allowances have steadily dropped as the relief load has increased and no provision is made for rents. There has been a determined opposition on the part of taxpayers' organizations to increasing relief appropriations which can only be carried by an increase in the tax on real estate. . . . Since April, when private funds were exhausted, the main burden of relief has been carried by the special state appropriation which was exhausted in July.

July expenditures were only $120,000 as compared to over a million dollars in June, 1932, because of this shortage. The city machinery for relief lapsed for two months until additional state funds were appropriated. Federal funds were finally made available in September.

Other Cities Desperate

Pittsburgh likewise has an increasingly serious problem with 178,000 unemployed and 30,000 on part time work, and relief expenditures for 1932 about three times that of 1931 although grants have been seriously reduced. Emergency appropriations from city and county have permitted relief to continue when state funds were exhausted. A work relief program ran from November, 1931, to March, 1932, during which time over

$1,000,000 raised by private subscription was expended for employment.

In Washington, D.C., a division of emergency relief was established in the board of public welfare during August, 1932. During this first month, applications came in at the rate of 200 and 300 a day, amounting to 7500 applications by the end of the month. Since only $60,000 a month is available until the next Congress meets and the load has been increasing, it has been necessary to cut the rate of relief about 40 per cent in order to take care of the increasing numbers. Work relief is being given through a private agency with the public department referring their clients for work on a case work basis. The Community Chest in Washington has also been forced to cut its budget 10 per cent, hoping that this deficiency will be met by a grant from Congress.

. . . . .

Million Unemployed in New York

New York City has a huge relief program with 1,000,000 of the city's 3,200,000 working population unemployed. Relief has been given on a "Disaster Basis" with disastrous effects on the population. Expenditures are running about $6,000,000 per month. The need is growing and $75,000,000 is considered a conservative estimate for the next twelve months. Combined city and state resources have been necessary to meet these needs.

In up-state New York the municipalities have been extremely fortunate in having the able assistance and financial support of the state temporary emergency relief administration. The state refunds 40 per cent of the money spent for outdoor relief and a proportion of the expenditures made for work relief in the local communities. In all of these cities the amount spent for 1932 is two or three times as great as for the corresponding period in 1931.

Buffalo expects its present funds to last until December 1, 1932, when it will raise enough on a bond issue to carry through the present fiscal year ending July 1, 1933. . . .

In Rochester the public welfare department spent its 1932 budget in less than five months. The economy program of the city administration and legal restrictions on the amount of money raised for current expenses have hampered the program.

In Syracuse the public welfare department budget was exhausted in September. The food allowance had been reduced to 11 cents per person per day. Housing congestion has intensified and living standards were lowered. The expenditures for outright and wage relief had almost tripled during the year. . . .

. . . . .

Conditions in industrial centers in the south are also serious. In Birmingham, Alabama, there were 12,000 tax delinquencies and there had been 6,000 tax sales by the first of the year. Although the city has been paying for the relief given, this has been administered by the Red Cross. The food allowance has been less than $4.00 a week for a family. City and county treasuries were in such serious condition that additional funds could not be made available in August. In certifying their needs to the R.F.C., the governor gave supporting data to show this, also their lack of power to issue or assume obligations and the lack of market for such obligations if issued. As a result of this extreme situation, $225,000 was made available to the city of Birmingham and county of Jefferson to meet these current relief needs.

Depression Hits the West

Although the west was slower to feel the effects of the depression than other sections, it is now fully sharing the general situation. In Denver the city's charity budget for 1932 was exhausted by the end of April. The mayor turned over an additional $1,000,000 to last until September 1. The special unemployment fund of $452,700 which was raised by private subscription last November was exhausted by spring and the committee $100,000 in debt by the time an additional $175,000 was raised. During July, 1932, a total of $61,056 was spent which represented an increase of

157.5 per cent over July, 1931. Work relief in the form of lumber camps accounted for nearly $12,000 of this expenditure.

On the west coast, Portland, Seattle, San Francisco and Los Angeles are all having their difficulties. Seattle (King County) has had $675,000 made available by the R.F.C. Supporting data accompanying the application of the governor estimated the needs of King County during September, October, and November at $1,375,000. Of this total, $600,000 will be covered by local governmental funds and $100,000 by private contributions in addition to the $675,000 from federal funds. Without this aid relief would have depended upon their ability to cash warrants and such warrants were selling at a large discount when application to the R.F.C. was made. The amount expended for relief in July, 1932, was $187,518 as compared to $26,483 in July, 1931, representing an increase a little over 600 per cent. Constitutional difficulties make it impossible for the state to assist at this time.

Portland, Oregon, has nearly 40,000 unemployed and over 13,000 families on relief. Of the $170,442 for relief given there during July, $124,112 was in the form of work relief.

Last winter Los Angeles had more than 150,000 unemployed, of whom 60,000 were heads of families. Funds have been running low so that the amount spent for relief in July, 1932, was actually 71.2 per cent less than that spent during July, 1931. Los Angeles has recently voted a $12,000,000 bond issue to meet this situation. The transient problem has complicated relief in Los Angeles to an unusual extent. The total relief for the San Francisco area in July, 1932, was $610,110 as compared to $166,441 in July, 1931, or an increase of nearly 300 per cent. A large proportion of this is given in the form of work relief. San Francisco has recently voted a bond issue of $6,500,000 to meet these increasing expenditures.

Lack of space prohibits discussion of similarly critical situations in many more cities. Enough has been said, however, to emphasize that we are struggling with a national calamity, occasioned by forces and circumstances above and beyond the control of municipalities. It has been demonstrated that national assistance on an increasing scale is a necessity if the financial integrity of municipalities is to be safeguarded and if relief is to be "furnished for needy and distressed people."

22 / REACTIONS TO DEPRESSION

Reports and statistics of suffering, while impressive enough, do not have the impact of individual stories. The following selections illustrate three of the startling developments of the early months of the Great Depression: Communist efforts to create a revolutionary situation, apple selling, and the appearance of the "Hooverville."

PHILADELPHIA REDS STORM CITY HALL

Philadelphia, Feb. 14—City Hall Plaza became a battleground soon after noon today when about 250 members of communistic organizations began a demonstration designed to point out, according to its leaders, that "while the manufacturers are reaping huge profits and Mayor Mackey goes on vacation trips there are 200,000 unemployed workers in the city of Philadelphia."

During a fifteen-minute engagement with 150 patrolmen, detectives and mounted policemen two of the paraders were sent to hospitals and seventeen were arrested.

Detective Lieutenant Jacob Gomborrow, in charge of the radical squad, informed Superintendent Mills at 11 o'clock this morning that the demonstration, originally planned for Feb. 26, had been moved up to coincide with the return of Mayor Mackey from a trip to the West Indies.

When the marchers left the headquarters of the Trade Union Unity League forty-five minutes later, they were escorted by a

SOURCE: *The New York Times,* February 15, 1930; November 6, 1930; November 14, 1930; November 12, 1930.

troop of mounted policemen who had been instructed to "lay off" until the order was given for action.

Arrived at City Hall, the paraders, including both men and women, who carried placards reading, "Organize and Fight," "We Want Work" and "Down With Politicians," formed a wide circle and sang the "Internationale." The next part of the plan, it was said, was to have a group ascend the stairs to interview Mayor Mackey, who had watched the demonstration from a window of his office.

As the crowd shouted, "To the Mayor, to the Mayor!" and as some of its members rushed forward, the police went into action. As clubs and fists were swung, several persons went down, including Assistant Superintendent of Police James Hearn, but by the end of fifteen minutes all the demonstrators who were not loaded into three patrol wagons had scattered.

Left behind were a battalion of disheveled policemen and a quantity of literature which had been intended for distribution. It called attention to a plan of the Communist party to stage unemployment demonstrations in every city in the country on Feb. 26, and added: "Have all the unemployed join councils of the Trade Union Unity League and join the demonstration at factory gates and civic centers."

Those who were taken to the hospitals for treatment later joined their companions in City Hall police cells to await a hearing tomorrow morning. . . .

Superintendent Mills said tonight that Philadelphia police ordinarily tried to ignore "these Reds," but that "when they deliberately began to attack officers and incite to riot it is a different matter."

E. Gardos, district organizer for the Communist party in this district, said the demonstration was organized by the Council of Unemployed of the Trade Union Unity League.

Magistrate Lifts Ban on Street Peddlers

Until the unemployment situation has passed, there is no such offence, so far as he is concerned, as peddling without a license, declared Magistrate Maurice H. Gotlieb last night in night court, as he arranged for seven men, who had been brought before him for vagrancy, to sell apples on the sidewalks. Six of the men were arrested in the Hudson Terminal and the seventh at Seventy-fourth Street and Madison Avenue for soliciting alms.

Magistrate Gotlieb suspended sentence on the seven men and asked them if they were willing to work. They said they were. The magistrate asked if they were willing to sell apples, and they agreed. The magistrate then gave them each $1 for a fund to start in business. One of the men inquired about a license.

"Times are too hard," the magistrate said. "Henceforth I will find guilty no one brought before me charged with peddling without a license."

One of the men, John Gervelac, 22 years old, of 2 East Seventy-eighth Street, said that he and his wife had not eaten for several days and that he wanted to get $2 so they could get food. He said that soon after marrying, in April, he lost his job, and had since supported himself and his wife by selling his blood for transfusion purposes.

Denies Apple Men Profit on Jobless

Despite vague muttering from various sources about racketeers pushing the price of apples from $1.75 to $2.25 a box since the sidewalks of New York began to sprout apple peddlers recruited from the ranks of the unemployed, the business continued to grow yesterday. It has been estimated that there are 4,000 to 6,000 men and women in it now, buying about $10,000 worth of apples a day.

Joseph Sicker, Chairman of the unemployed relief committee of the International Apple Shippers' Association, denied emphatically last night that he or any of the men connected with the venture was in it for personal gain. He insisted that the steady rise in the price of apples had resulted directly from the corner peddling of the unemployed—that the business had grown more rapidly than his organization anticipated.

"When we started this thing at the beginning of National Apple Week we had no idea that it would expand in this way," Sicker said. "We had a fund of approximately $10,000, donated by various men in the produce business, which we hoped would take care of the loss we would have to stand by selling these apples to the unemployed below the market price. But the simple law of supply and demand has reacted against the movement in forcing up the price."

The apples are distributed in crates containing 80, 88 or 100. He showed the daily fruit auction tables which indicated that the boxes of 100 apples which he was selling for $2 were listed at $2.20 a box, less the 7 cents which the committee must pay for cartage.

As he spoke a pale-faced boy on crutches hobbled over, removed his hat and asked if he could have a box of apples on credit. He had a man outside who had promised to cart the box to a busy corner uptown. Mr. Sicker shouted an order to one of the helpers on the warehouse floor and the crippled boy followed the box into West Street.

Abner Sicker, a brother of the committee chairman, described the various types that come in for credit and from his pocket drew two gold watches which had been left with him by "two fine-looking men who had been out of work a long time and wanted to get a start selling apples." He said he had told the men to keep the timepieces but they had insisted he hold them as evidence of their good faith.

Whether racketeering has wormed its way into the movement, there is no doubt that the apple-selling crusade has brought to thousands of men and women the first money they had earned in many months. Wherever the little boxes of apples stand the listener has no trouble getting from the vender the story of a long period of unemployment, misery at home and of near-starvation.

Mr. Sicker said last night that he understood that next week the apple-peddling movement for the unemployed would spread to Chicago, St. Louis and other large cities.

Chicago Jobless Colonize

Chicago, Nov. 11—Hooverville, so-called by a colony of unemployed men, has sprung up in Chicago's front yard at the foot of Randolph Street near Grant Park, like one of the mushroom mining towns of bonanza days of the Far West.

A primitive form of government has been set up in this "shanty town" and Mike Donovan, a disabled former railroad brakeman and miner is "Mayor" by common consent. It has its Prosperity Road, Easy Street and Hard Times Avenue, all crudely labelled.

The shacks are built of discarded materials. The "Mayor's" residence at the corner of Prosperity Road, and Easy Street, is made of brick, wood and sheet iron.

"Building construction may be at a standstill elsewhere, but down here everything is booming," said "Mayor" Donovan today. "Ours is a sort of communistic government. We pool our interests and when the commissary shows signs of depletion, we appoint a committee to see what leavings the hotels have."

23 / ENFORCED MASS LEISURE

Tam Deering, director of recreation for Cincinnati, finds that the Great Depression has vastly increased the demands upon his department at the same time that the funds available for its work have been reduced.

Brief Statement of Activities of the Public Recreation Commission for the Year 1932

The worth of all activities of our City Government may be measured in the extent to which they make living in Cincinnati more enjoyable and worthwhile for everybody.

In 1932 our people came into possession of a vast amount of enforced leisure, and they found themselves for the most part without any adequate education how to use this leisure constructively. A conspicuous example of the disrupting effect of no work and no understanding how to use leisure time is to be observed in the hundreds of thousands of young men and boys who are wandering about the country.

Through its Public Recreation Commission, Cincinnati has striven to meet this need.

Twenty thousand different people have registered and participated regularly in municipal athletics: 7,000 in recreation ball, 5,000 in baseball, 4,500 in tennis, 2,000 in basketball, 1,000 in golf, and 748 in track. Thirteen thousand of these were adults.

Seven indoor recreation centers, managed especially for the unemployed, have drawn tens of thousands of men throughout the year.

SOURCE: "Sixth Annual Report of the Public Recreation Commission, Cincinnati, Ohio, January 1, 1932, to December 31, 1932," n.d., n.p. (mimeographed).

The Cincinnati Civic Orchestra, made up of eighty amateur players, and a number of neighborhood orchestras have been maintained under excellent leadership to give opportunity for musical activity for non-professional musicians, while innumerable groups have been assisted in finding recreation through music in community singing.

Community centers maintained at a number of schools have been operated in cooperation with neighborhood organizations.

The City has recognized the strain on its children and the harmfulness and blocking of the children's growth resulting from a home atmosphere of gloom and worry because of unemployment and insecurity, and has undertaken to offset this by maintaining greater numbers of playcenters and playgrounds where the development of the children—mentally, socially and physically—would be facilitated by a wholesome activity in an environment that radiates joy and happiness.

When the schools were forced to close two weeks earlier, the City took responsibility and operated its playgrounds two weeks earlier. Nearly 35,000 children were reached at the fifty playgrounds and playcenters, an increase of 11% over any previous year.

Acting on the suggestion of the City Manager and at the request of the Welfare Department, the Public Recreation Commission has furnished employment to 2,000 men working on two day shifts each week over a period of many months.

Private citizens have contributed $5,000 in cash and have donated or loaned $10,000 worth of equipment toward this undertaking of effecting permanent improvements. The construction work has been carried on at fifteen different locations where playgrounds are being constructed or improved. At Coy Athletic Field, a $12,000 unit of hard-surfaced tennis courts has been constructed without any expenditure by the City except the relief given to the unemployed men who performed the labor. At the "C & O" Playground and Athletic Field, between Third and Fourth Streets, playing areas and facilities which would have cost $35,000 on contract have been developed without expenditure of a penny of City funds, except such as was given in relief to the unemployed men on the job.

A great increase in the City's playing areas in many parts of the City has been brought about through the use of the labor of the unemployed men. No project has been undertaken by the Public Recreation Commission unless it has conformed to five requirements: (1) A well selected site. (2) Properly designed plan prepared by a competent landscape architect. (3) Supervision of a competent Superintendent of Construction. (4) A sufficient supply of tools and equipment. (5) A well directed campaign to interest the laborers in the work they were doing.

Besides adding to the City's playing areas, the Public Recreation Commission has been especially interested in giving the 2,000 men work to do of a character that would improve their physical health and their morale. It has keenly realized the demoralization which comes to men, and especially to those who are heads of families, as result of enforced idleness accompanied by a feeling of uselessness and constant state of worry. Important as is the increase of playing areas, the Commission believes that an even greater social value may be observed in the greater meaning and interest which has been given to the lives of the 2,000 men as a result of their being engaged in the construction of something of greatest importance to their own children and to their fellow citizens.

In 1932 the municipal recreation budget was $10,000 less than the 1931 budget and $20,000 less than the 1930 budget. Nevertheless, there has been at least a twenty percent increase in the services rendered.

24 / THE COMPLEXITY OF URBAN GOVERNMENT

Three political scientists, Charles E. Merriam, Spencer D. Parratt, and Albert Lepawsky, find that governing a huge city like Chicago is a nearly impossible task. Power and responsibility are dispersed far too widely, they learn, for effective government.

The governmental confusion in the Chicago Area begins at the center and extends to the circumference. The city corporate of Chicago, the County of Cook, and the whole region illustrate progressively the stages in the decentralization and disintegration of government in this great community.

A look at central Chicago and a look at Cook County may well precede the analysis of the region as a whole.

The city of Chicago itself contains within its limits no less than 27 independent taxing bodies, including the greater part of three large agencies—the County of Cook, the Sanitary District, and the Forest Preserve District. Twenty of the 27 governments including the city corporate, the Board of Education, the Lincoln Park, West Park, and South Park districts, and 15 minor park districts are entirely within the city limits. Foremost is, of course, the city of Chicago with its elective council and mayor. The Municipal Tuberculosis Sanitarium is a separate body with an independent tax rate but is fairly well controlled through ap-

SOURCE: Charles E. Merriam, Spencer D. Parratt, and Albert Lepawsky, "The Twenty-Seven Governments to the Inner City of Chicago," *The Government of the Metropolitan Region of Chicago* (Chicago: University of Chicago Press, 1933), pp. 19–23. Reprinted by permission of The University of Chicago Press.

pointment by the mayor, as is the board of inspectors of the House of Correction.

The Board of Education consists of 11 members who are appointed by the mayor for five-year terms, but not removable by him, and may go on their own independent way, financially and otherwise—and do from time to time. But their expenditures, at one time approaching $100,000,000 a year, and their basic interests are intimately related to the life of Chicago. The Public Library Board, with 9 members, is likewise appointed by the mayor, and has its own independent budget.

The 3 large park boards—South, West, and Lincoln—and 19 smaller ones are wholly independent of the city, although the recreation problem is primarily one that interests the whole community. The Lincoln Park and West Park boards are appointed by the governor of the state, and raise and spend their own funds without any control whatever from Chicago. The South Park Board is appointed by the judges of the Circuit Court of Cook County, and is likewise entirely independent of the municipality of Chicago. The 19 small park commissions are elected in small districts and enjoy complete autonomy from the city. The annual budget of these Boards has been around $5,000,000.

The Sanitary District of Chicago, organized primarily to deal with Chicago's sewage problem, is governed by a board of 9 trustees elected by the voters of the District which now has jurisdiction over territory including 60 suburban cities and villages in Cook County in addition to Chicago. Its annual budget, which has exceeded seventy million dollars, is expended by the trustees (sometimes with catastrophic results) without any control by the City. The District has acquired renown in extravagance of expenditure and in political irresponsibility, but it should also be known for the scope of its undertakings. Established in 1889–90 with an area of 185 square miles, an assessed valuation of only $217,000,000, and an annual expenditure of less than $70,000, it has grown to over 440 square miles, with an assessed valuation of almost $4,500,000,000 in 1930 and a budget of $73,946,000 in 1931. Up to 1932, it had expended the sum of $300,000,000, and its future construction plan alone calls for the outlay of $20,000,000 per year for the next four years. Originally the District was an agency almost entirely concerned with the city of Chicago. Ninety-two per cent of its area and 96 per cent of its population was found within the city in 1890. Now but 48 per cent of its area and 86 per cent of its population and its wealth is in the city. The District has expanded from its original size to a government of metropolitan proportions and of Regional significance.

Finally comes Cook County, with 85 per cent of its population and 84 per cent of its wealth lying within the boundaries of the city of Chicago; but Cook County is an entirely independent taxing and governing body. Its 15 county commissioners administer important affairs within the limits of the city. Its assessing authorities value the property of the city and collect its taxes. Its sheriff and deputies are independent of the city police force. It administers public welfare services for the county. Its county judge passes upon important problems of Chicago, not the least of which are election affairs, administered by a Board of Election Commissioners, chosen by him.

The government of the inner Chicago is thus a combination of 7 main agencies, each of which raises and spends money, each of which administers affairs of very grave importance in the life of the community—schools, parks, water and sewage, welfare and justice, taxation; all these are in the city but not of it. All these agencies distribute and divide the central functions of local government among them.

To this there must be added the municipal court with judges to the number of 37, together with a chief clerk and bailiff, all elected by the voters of Chicago, but not under the control of the city government. The finances and administration of this court are independent of the municipality, and attempted control on the part of the city of Chicago is almost always zealously resisted by the judicial group.

If we extend the lines somewhat farther out to include all of Cook County, we find the confusion growing greater as the limits are extended. The County of Cook has a population of 3,982,123 in an area of 933 square miles, with property to the taxable value of $4,516,485,826 (1930). The number of independent governments in this area reaches the total of 419.

The government of the county consists of a board of 15 commissioners (10 from Chicago and 5 outside) and a series of 13 elective offices, surviving from a half-century ago. Nor does this include 20 Circuit Court judges, 28 Superior Court judges, a county judge, and a judge of the Probate Court. The Forest Preserve District, a park district primarily intended to take care of the outer belt park system of Chicago, is coterminous with the county, but is an independent unit composed of the county commissioners acting ex officio and with separate financial authority.

But this is only the beginning of county complexity, for we must now include the Sanitary District of Chicago, the 20 governments totally within Chicago, and the 4 park districts sprawling across the city's borders. Then we must take notice of 88 municipalities scattered through the county area outside Chicago, of 30 townships, of 194 school districts, of 34 small park districts, of 3 sanitary and 40 drainage districts, of 2 mosquito-abatement districts, 1 health district, all within the limits of the County of Cook.

An effort was made to introduce some element of unity into the government of the county by building up the powers of the president of the County Board through the veto power and through a range of appointing power. To some extent this attempt was successful in emphasizing the importance of greater unity in the scattered affairs of Cook County. But this unit is still greatly disorganized. It remains with a central board of 15, and alongside it a series of 13 elective offices chosen by the voters and not responsible to the Board. This list includes the state's attorney, the sheriff, the recorder, the coroner, the treasurer, the county superintendent of schools, the county clerk, the clerks of the Circuit, Superior, Probate, Criminal and Appellate courts, and even the county surveyor, each of whom is independent of all the others and of the Board itself in most matters. The duties and responsibilities of these officials are largely set forth in the statutes of the state and the constitution, and they are not subject to the administrative supervision of the County Board or of its president.

To increase the confusion and irresponsibility, the judges of the Circuit Court of Cook County, 20 in number, have the singular authority, conferred by the Illinois Constitution itself, to fix the number of employees in the county fee offices, while the compensation of these employees is determined by the County Board. With the best of intentions the framers of this constitutional provision set up what proved to be a formula of confusion in county finance.

Nor are the numerous towns or other minor subdivisions of the county subject to central control by the officials of the county with some exceptions, as in the case of schools. But in the main the 419 governments are free to pursue their own way, independent of any effective supervision.

The central core of the city government is simple beside the disintegration of the government of Cook County. Adapted perhaps to the needs of a rural community a half-century ago, the county has completely outgrown its bounds, and stands as a classic type of disorganization, so grotesque from the point of view of administration that no one could even have imagined so absurd a caricature of responsible government.

25 / A DAY IN THE LIFE OF THE POLICE COMMISSIONER

Another of Chicago's perennial problems was that of its law enforcement agencies. How difficult it was for the police commissioner to give effective leadership is illustrated in a report prepared for one of that city's periodic citizens' reform associations.

It is 9:00 A.M. The police commissioner is at his desk. A secretary enters with the morning mail. There is not much of it, the great bulk having been withheld for answer by the secretary. Later in the day the commissioner will perfunctorily affix his signature to a considerable sheaf of correspondence.

A visitor is shown in. He is an alderman from the "Great West Side." He has come on behalf of a patrolman suspended from duty pending action by the civil service Trial Board. The commissioner shows signs of exasperation until it appears that the alderman has already seen the mayor's personal representative. The conversation becomes earnest and is conducted in lower and lower tones. Five minutes elapse, and the alderman emerges through a door, always open, which leads into a small anteroom.

His place beside the commissioner's desk is taken by the business agent of a traveling circus. He wants to have fifty policemen assigned to the circus ground and its immediate vicinity during the coming week; at public expense, of course. He, too, has "seen" somebody and confidently presents his case. The

SOURCE: The Citizens' Police Committee, *Chicago Police Problems* (Chicago: University of Chicago Press, 1931), pp. 29–35. Reprinted by permission of University of Chicago Press. Copyright 1931 by The University of Chicago.

commissioner wonders how he can satisfy this request and many others of a similar nature without reducing uniformed patrols to the vanishing-point. True, the patrol of private property is no part of a police department's public responsibility, but he cannot very well offend the circus agent's sponsor. So he presents a counter proposal. There is some haggling, and a detail of twenty policemen is finally agreed upon.

Next to enter is an alderman who is also a member of the City Council's Finance Committee. He has a grievance, since police officers on duty in his ward are making things uncomfortable for persons in illicit callings who expect to secure "protection" from their alderman. The police commissioner makes a gallant stand. He tells the alderman that no political influence can be permitted to interfere with the performance of police duty. The alderman retires in some discomfiture, which the commissioner seems to enjoy. But there will come another day when the commissioner will appear before the Finance Committee of the Council on behalf of his annual estimates. This alderman will make sure to be present, and perhaps the commissioner will then regret the courage and independence which he has just shown. Next time he may be more cautious and will trade with the alderman instead of giving cause for offense.

Meanwhile, the small anteroom is filling up. Soon there will be nothing but standing room, and very little of that, for those who wish to see the commissioner. Most of them are well known around the City Hall. There are aldermen, ward-heelers, bail-bondsmen, police characters, and a few ranking police officers. The latter will have to take their turn. Some of those present have gained admission to the anteroom without passing through the general reception room and stating their business to the commissioner's secretary. They have pass keys which admit them directly from the corridor outside. So they are privileged characters.

The stream of visitors continues to pass into the commissioner's private office by ones, twos, threes. From time to time this stream is interrupted by the appearance of a familiar figure. Presumably he comes from the mayor's office, which is immediately adjacent to that of the commissioner. At all events he is the mayor's messenger, and he brings orders from some higher authority. The contents of these orders are unknown. They are never published.

Outside, in a large reception room, the general public awaits its turn to see the commissioner. The wait will be a long one. Many will become discouraged and leave. A few will persist and finally secure an interview. They represent the commissioner's sole direct contact with the public which he serves. All of the others are representatives of special groups and interests, for the most part political.

Occasionally an officeholder or ward-leader enters the reception room. He does not require to see the commissioner; the secretary will suffice. He has a number of traffic-violation slips which have been issued to some of his constituents by traffic police. These must be "fixed" if the politician's repute as a power at City Hall is to be maintained back in his ward. No time is wasted. The secretary receives the violation notices, places them in an envelope, already near full, and files the latter in a pigeonhole above his desk. This is efficiency.

Returning to the commissioner's office, we find him in conference with a police personnel inspector. The latter has been assigned to investigate graft charges laid against certain police officers on the North Side. Evidence has been secured which will warrant formal charges and an administrative trial, but it appears that the police under suspicion have important connections. It is all very complicated.

The luncheon hour arrives and the anteroom is still full. The commissioner comes out of his private office and makes his way through the throng. It requires several minutes for him to traverse the length of the anteroom, about fifteen feet. He holds quick, whispered conferences, now to the right, now to the left. Some he puts off with a noncommittal statement. These will come back after they have fortified their positions by seeing the right person. To others the commissioner gives quick acquiescence; they also will come back, though after a longer lapse of time and on a different errand.

The door to the corridor finally gained, the commissioner

takes with him one or two of the most importunate. They will lunch together at a nearby restaurant, where the conferences will continue. The waiting crowd thins out, but it will congregate again before the commissioner's return.

The afternoon hours go by in much the same fashion. News reporters drop in to inquire concerning the status of the latest murder mystery. They already know, of course, and the commissioner probably does not. He has been too busy with interviews. However, the press must have a statement, and the commissioner, by referring to the teletype tape and the daily reports of divisional commanders, can usually make some kind of a statement. If a suspect has been locked up, so much the better. The commissioner is forced to think in terms of news headlines. He cannot ignore the advantages of publicity.

Now comes the manager of a local theater, whose current attraction has been prohibited by the police censors, represented in most cases by a policewoman. The manager profanely inquires concerning what the police know about "art." The commissioner has not seen the performance, but as the last administrative court of appeal, except for the mayor, he must pronounce what is virtually a final judgment. So the hours pass.

It is late afternoon, and the anteroom is at last vacant but for a handful of police officers. They are the commissioner's "kitchen cabinet," who have been informally selected because of their personal qualifications and unquestioned loyalty. With the commissioner they constitute a Board of Strategy. All of the large problems confronting the Police Department, and many others of lesser importance, are considered by this group. Their ranks and duties are various. Including a deputy commissioner or two, a bureau chief, a section supervisor, and perhaps a police captain, they are all equal here. Their daily routine has been performed, and they are gathered now in advisory session. The press of visitors has ceased, and at last the decks are cleared for the real business of police administration.

Many of the ranking officers of the Department are conspicuous by their absence. Police rank is secured through the civil service authorities, supported by occasional political influence.

It is not derived from the commissioner, and hence there is no necessary bond of loyalty.

The Board of Strategy convenes. There is talk of a large-scale "shakedown" by police in a South Side district. Nothing can be proved under the formal procedure of an administrative trial. The matter is finally resolved by transfer of the police district's entire personnel, from captain to patrolmen, to the four quarters of the city. It is so ordered.

The next subject for discussion involves a redistribution of man-power and equipment in order to meet a supposed crime emergency. Diverse opinions are expressed concerning the reality of the condition, and the man-power needs of this district or that. The commissioner wants facts, or at all events he should have them.

Before him lies an imposing file of daily reports covering various police activities. These embrace the preceding twenty-four hours, together with weekly cumulations in some instances. They represent the only regular means by which the commissioner can secure a larger view of his police force, its problems, and its work. If he turns to this source of information, he may chance upon the chief operator's daily teletype report. It informs him that "there was no trouble reported on the teletype for the twenty-four hours ending at 8:00 A.M., September 23, 19—." This is intended to convey the information that teletype service is continuing without interruption from mechanical or electrical causes. It is of little help. The next to catch his eye is a sheaf of forty-one dog-bite reports, one from each district. The daily formula has been mimeographed so as to avoid burdensome repetition. The first one reads, "No dog bites were reported in this district." The second, third, and many others carry the same reassurance.

Next is a sheaf of unmuzzled dog reports, also from forty-one districts. There follows a series of other documents, dealing with city and state vehicle tax violations, reports of the number of arrests for speeding in each police district, for overnight parking on public thoroughfares, and the like. A report from the captain commanding the central traffic zone informs the commissioner that there have been two accidents resulting in personal injury during the past twenty-four hours: "At Monroe and Dearborn, 8:30 A.M., September 25, Mrs. F——— M———, age twenty years, was struck by street car No. 652, run No. 151; taken to Iroquois Hospital; abrasions on left side of forehead, fingers, and both knees." The second accident is more serious, involving a fifty-five-year-old victim, who "was struck by ——— Cab operated by T——— S———; taken to Iroquois Hospital; cerebral concussion, possible skull fracture." Still, there is nothing here upon which the commissioner can act.

Somewhere in the file he will find the daily crime reports from the districts, which describe in considerable detail several of the outstanding offenses and important arrests occurring in each. These are supplemented by a weekly "summary of criminal complaints, raids, and important happenings." Nowhere in the commissioner's office is there a daily statistical summary of the distribution of available men and equipment, of offenses reported and the action taken thereon, or graphic charts showing current crime trends, and the effectiveness of the several police units.

So the Board of Strategy resumes its labors with nothing more than general impressions upon which to map its campaign. The members present offer suggestions from time to time. The commissioner listens attentively, because he can trust these advisers who are sitting here before him. They all know that the official favor which they are now enjoying will cease abruptly when the commissioner steps out of his office for the last time. Some of them will be informally, but none the less severely, disciplined for their intimate association with this commissioner. However, there is always a chance that a future administration will bring them back from minor assignments for these conferences at the City Hall.

It is early evening, and the meeting breaks up. The commissioner is tired, and little wonder. He has had a full day. Most of it has been expended in propitiating the various influences which put him into office, and which must be fortified if he is to continue there. Little time has been devoted to constructive work or police strategy. Perhaps if he could get away for a few weeks he might be able to think the thing through. No, the whole matter is too complicated to permit that. He must be at his desk every day and hold the line. A disturbing thought assails him. When he is finally forced out of office—experience teaches him that this will be only a matter of months—none of the public officials and politicians whom he is now obliging will utter a word of personal regret, or of praise for the public or private services he has rendered. They will be too busy repairing their political fences with which to hedge about his successor, and constructing a maze through which the latter must thread his way.

It is just as well for his peace of mind that he cannot see all of the acts of neglect and corruption committed by some of his subordinates. Only a few of the most flagrant instances will ever come to his attention. Even police headquarters is now unfamiliar ground to him. It is over a mile removed from his desk at the City Hall. In the field of actual police administration he is not an active force at all. He is merely a symbol.

PART V

New Hope for the City

THE advent of the New Deal brought hope to the desperate cities after three years of increasing distress. Early in the new administration, federal funds began to flow into the relief coffers. Even more important was the coming, in November, 1933, of the Civil Works Administration, a direct work relief program under federal direction. Its effect upon millions of Americans was electric; many received pay checks for the first time in years (Selection 26).

The mayors of the cities had been the first public officials to recognize, as a body, that only the national government could provide the necessary financial assistance to relieve their burdens. They welcomed the largess bestowed by the Roosevelt administration and asked for more (Selection 27). Bypassing state governments, which were often unsympathetic to urban needs, the mayors set the stage for a new development in American politics, the direct relationship of federal and municipal governments. Urban life was enriched in other ways by many New Deal projects. Post offices were decorated with murals, not always very good; children were taught the intricacies of modern dance; and, for the first time, the theater received support from public funds (Selection 28).

No section of the country was in greater need nor probably gained more from the federal treasury than the South. Southern leaders understandably did not always appreciate having attention brought to their region, as did a widely-read report which inspired the President to describe the South as "the Nation's No. 1 economic problem" (Selection 29).

Despite the vast amounts of money made available, however, permanent prosperity evaded the national government. A recession, during Roosevelt's second term, drastically increased the numbers of persons seeking relief (Selection 30).

The economic situation did improve, despite setbacks, and with it new political loyalties were created. In 1940 most American voters were prepared to defy the two-term tradition and again chose Franklin Roosevelt to lead them. The margin of victory for the Democrats clearly was to be found in the city (Selection 31).

26 / A DECENT RELIEF PROGRAM AT LAST

The significance of the first important federal work relief project, late in 1933, to city-dwellers can be seen in the following selection. Similar articles about other states and regions filled the Editorial Section of the Times *that Sunday, reflecting even that staid journal's rejoicing at the creation of the Civil Works Administration.*

Boston, Nov. 22. The Civil Works Program is going over with a bang in New England.

Sentiment in general is favorable to the plan as an emergency scheme. Many measures that would be condemned as foolish or reckless by the average thrifty Yankee in normal times are tolerated now. Every city in the six states has been looking for-

SOURCE: F. Lauriston Bullard, "Civil Works Plan Stirs New England," *The New York Times,* November 26, 1933.

ward with apprehension to the coming of Winter with an enormous amount of welfare work somehow to be done.

Any big job put through with such haste is liable to be bungled, at least to some extent. Politics must be kept out of both approvals and allocations. Every project must be officially adopted as "useful," not a mere makeshift but a permanent improvement, and fitting if it be possible into a comprehensive scheme of public works. Able men have to be chosen for the key positions of direction and supervision and their decisions on the questions that arise at the outset must be shrewdly made. In some cases these men have already withstood heavy pressure and maintained the rules as laid down from Washington and their own interpretations thereof.

With right good-will they have cut through the red-tape entanglements that have been as effective as barbed wire in slowing down the public works program authorized by the special session. There have been serious clashes of opinion also here in Boston and in many other cities as to what projects ought to be accepted for that public works program. Anyhow, after several months not a dollar has been received in Massachusetts under that program and not a man has been put to work. Compare this with the announcement that a million pay checks now are on the way from Washington for use in this new venture. To multitudes of men, weary with the hopeless quest of jobs, it all seems too good to be true. They have almost mobbed the city halls in many places.

Back from Washington on Thursday night last came four New England Governors and a score of Mayors, full of enthusiasm for the program which they had heard the President explain. It means for Massachusetts a grant of about $12,000,000 and employment until mid-February of about 100,000 men, half of whom it is hoped to have at work by the end of the present week. Governor Louis J. Brann of Maine estimates his quota will be 20,000 men; Governor Stanley C. Wilson of Vermont looks forward to 3,000, and Governor Winant of New Hampshire about the same number.

To the members of the Massachusetts Emergency Finance

Board, with Joseph W. Bartlett of Newton as chairman, whose duty it had been to examine and pass upon projects submitted for the Public Works Program, was assigned the duty of approving projects and allocating men under this Civil Works plan. They worked on the details all day Sunday and Monday morning were ready for the big meeting at the State House. The Governor outlined the idea and emphasized especially that all any city or town had to do is to report its proposals to the board and get its approval—and then go ahead. Instead of a series of submissions and approvals only one now is required. Chairman Bartlett then explained the Federal regulations, which he summarized thus: "Regular work at regular wages for unemployed persons able and willing to work. All projects to be done by day labor, no contracts, in a week of thirty hours, at 50 cents an hour for unskilled and $1.20 an hour for skilled labor. The men to be selected by heads of welfare departments in each community who would in each case be appointed as Civil Works Administrator."

A touch of the dramatic ensued. Up stepped the Mayor of Worcester and slapped a program on the table. In four hours it had been approved and he was on his way back home to get men on the job. Right on his heels the Mayor of Lowell came down the aisle with another program neatly drawn.

The total of civil works projects now approved and officially listed runs into hundreds in this State and into scores in the others. The amounts of money to be used on them runs from $5,700 for such a small town as Hull to $2,500,000 for Boston, $542,000 for Worcester and $449,000 for Springfield. In Rhode Island Governor Green expects that this plan means the transfer of some 9,000 men from relief rolls to these work projects. The story is simply the same with variations in the other States. Governor Brann has said that the first project he would push would be the creation of a Roosevelt park on Mount Katahdin, thus employing 3,000 men. In the main the projects thus far put forward include street building and repair, sewerage, work on public buildings, parks and playgrounds, and the like, which in the main have been long contemplated and delayed from lack of funds.

27 / CITY-FEDERAL COOPERATION

At the 1935 meeting of the United States Conference of Mayors, the chief executives of American cities adopted a series of resolutions calling upon the federal government to expand its aid to the beleaguered municipalities.

For a Long-Range Program of Public Works and Relief

Whereas, the problem of relief is of the utmost importance to every city administration; and

Whereas, it has been the experience of every city that without Federal aid the situation could not have been met; and

Whereas, a careful survey indicates that, regardless of business and industrial improvement, all employable men and women cannot possibly be permanently re-employed, so that for some time to come, and particularly pending such time as adequate national security measures will become effective, it will be necessary to provide and care for such of our fellow citizens who are unable to find gainful employment; and

Whereas, we have learned from experience that greater efficiency can be obtained and economy effected by a longer-range program for relief work instead of month-to-month allocations; and

Whereas, city budgets are planned on a yearly basis and effective cooperation can be rendered if Federal relief and work policies could be synchronized to such budget years;

Therefore be it resolved that the United States Conference of Mayors express their appreciation and gratitude to the President

SOURCE: "Better Federal-Municipal Cooperation Urged," *The American City,* L (December, 1935), 5.

of the United States and to the Congress for their vision and courage in establishing in an unprecedented manner the policy of Federal aid for destitute, unemployed persons; and

Be it further resolved that the United States Conference of Mayors petition Congress for additional appropriations for the fiscal year 1936–1937 sufficient to meet a planned and comprehensive program for relief work and direct aid to meet the unemployment situation throughout the country for such period; and

Be it further resolved that the President of this Conference and the Executive Committee be and are hereby authorized to cooperate with Congress and to appear before such committees of the House and Senate of the United States Congress that may be considering legislation and appropriations for relief purposes and present to them the needs of the cities and the estimates for further requirements, and the need for the continuance of President Roosevelt's policy of Federal aid for relief purposes; and

Be it further resolved that a copy of this resolution be forwarded to the President of the United States, to the Vice-President of the United States and the President pro tem. of the Senate, Speaker of the House of Representatives, and that each mayor send to the representatives in Congress of the district in which his city is located a copy of this resolution.

Cooperation and Contributions from States

Whereas, it is the judgment of this Conference that in order adequately, scientifically, and humanely to meet the problem of unemployment it is necessary to continue work relief and direct relief; and

Whereas, cities and states should join with the Federal Government in providing the necessary funds, and legislatures must make the necessary appropriations to care for the states' apportionment or give adequate authority to the municipalities to provide funds to insure the cooperative effort of these three levels of government;

Therefore be it resolved that the cities take proper steps to insure adequate and proper cooperation and contribution from their own states; and

Be it further resolved that in order to obtain the full force, effect, and benefit of national social security legislation and appropriation, such legislation must be nation-wide and in every state of the union. To that end mayors should contact their governors and state legislators to obtain the necessary state action to come within the purview, scope, and benefits of national security laws, and adopt the present uniform law as suggested by the Department of Labor in keeping with the statutes.

Low-Cost Housing and Slum Clearance

Whereas, there has been a great deal of public attention to the question of a public housing program, though relatively little has been accomplished on such a program; and

Whereas, an extensive housing plan on a nation-wide scale would give strength and stability to the economic structure of the nation; and

Whereas, numerous surveys and studies of housing conditions throughout the country indicate the growing shortage and congestion in housing facilities; and

Whereas, the disgraceful conditions in city slums and country hovels have a directly detrimental effect on the social well-being of these areas and the surrounding communities; and

Whereas, it is obvious that the Federal Government must assume the financing of such self-liquidating projects through loans or investments and low interest rates;

Now, therefore be it resolved that the United States Conference of Mayors does hereby urge upon Congress and the President the vital importance of this problem and the need for a well-coordinated and extensive housing program for the so-called low-income group, where desired and the need exists; and

Further, that the United States Conference of Mayors lend its assistance to the preparation and realization of such a program which will be substantially financed by the Federal Government, though in the interest of economy and efficiency the responsibility for the administration of the specific projects of the program be in the hands of the local authorities where so desired.

Relief for Transients

Whereas, the problem of providing relief for transients is a peculiarly national or Federal problem; and

Whereas, the municipalities are unable to handle adequately the problem of relief to transient persons and non-residents;

Therefore be it resolved that the United States Conference of Mayors request a continuing program of Federal transient relief to the end that provision be made for the relief of transients.

Municipal Employees and Old-Age Security

Whereas, municipal employees are not included under the provisions of the Social Security Act except that they would be eligible for old-age assistance if in need after retirement; and

Whereas, it is entirely possible, and we believe highly desirable, that provision be made whereby municipalities desiring to provide old-age security for their employees may come under the national system;

Therefore be it resolved that the United States Conference of Mayors petition the President and the Congress to amend the Social Security Law so as to enable municipalities, on a voluntary basis, to participate in the above manner.

28 / PUBLIC SUPPORT FOR THE THEATER

Rosamond Gilder, an editor of Theatre Arts Monthly *and an official of the Federal Theatre Project, Works Progress Administration, reports on the first few months of the brief, but exciting, time when the stage received financial support from the federal government.*

Six months ago Federal Theatre was a theory, a plan, a wild surmise. Today it is a far-flung reality with two hundred producing groups and a personnel of over 12,000—one of the largest government-supported theatres in the world. Its New York record to date shows seven major productions of which four have played to full houses. Fifty-seven per cent success is a high average in a business that accepts seventy-three per cent of failures in a season, but to compare Broadway and Federal Theatre in anything but the most general terms is unfair to both. Federal Theatre could never produce an *Idiot's Delight*; Broadway could never sell, at a fifty-five cent top, so beautiful and dignified a production as that given T. S. Eliot's *Murder in the Cathedral*. The costs of Federal Theatre productions cannot be reckoned on the same balance sheet as those of the commercial producer. Where Federal Theatre has the advantage of a fixed salary scale, set for all WPA workers alike, it has the disadvantage of having little or no choice in casting; it cannot hire and fire at will, its working hours per day are short and it must make up by long and patient rehearsals for the inequalities in its acting groups.

The salary scale is low, according to union minimums, but few producing organizations in America pay salaries month in and

SOURCE: Rosamond Gilder, "The Federal Theatre, A Record," *Theatre Arts Monthly*, XX (June, 1936), 430–38.

month out, whether a play is in rehearsal or performance, whether it is a hit or a flop. Security wage, while rightly small, has the value of such certainty as Congress and Appropriation bills afford, but when laid end to end over weeks of organization, try-outs and rehearsals the sums paid to the workers in Federal Theatre would be difficult for private producers to match. This applies equally to work in the shops and offices of this relief-run organization. Salaries are low, actual costs of materials are kept at a minimum, every effort is made in the Federal Theatre workshop, in the Treasury and Procurement Divisions, to buy as cheaply and wisely as possible, but when it comes to figuring out the exact cost of a production a fair picture is difficult to achieve. Since the Federal Theatre is established for the purpose of providing employment for those on home relief, regardless of their speed or efficiency, many more people must be carried on the payroll than would be needed if only the most experienced workers were employed.

All this is merely to reiterate an obvious truth: Federal Theatre cannot and should not be evaluated on a bookkeeping basis because its reason for being is not theatre, but unemployment, not business or even art, but just plain necessity. Today, as this goes to press, Congress is in hot dispute over the wisdom of the various methods for taking care of this need. The dole and work relief, the preservation of skills, technological unemployment, white collar projects and heavy construction plans, WPA and PWA techniques are being fought over in the newspapers, in Congress, in every place where two or three are gathered to argue, view with alarm or take action on the state of the nation. This is no place to enter into that poignant argument.

Leaders in the Federal Theatre accepted the situation as they found it when they took up their challenging tasks six months ago. The Four Arts projects had been established. Millions of dollars were to be spent in wages for unemployed theatre workers who were to be set to work on the theatre project. Millions had already been spent in the same field by various state administrators. In September 1935 the question was whether anything more constructive, forward-looking, alive, worth while, could be done with the millions of dollars, the thousands of skills that were required to be employed during the year. The question today is: How far does the record accord with the prophecy? What has happened to the vision in the face of reality?

To this degree they accord perfectly: wherever Federal Theatre has been able to carry out its Director's original plan it has been signally successful. Wherever that plan has been frustrated by the slings and arrows of a variety of outrageous fortunes, political and human, it has made no mark. Both in its successes and in its failures, Federal Theatre proved the solid sense that lay behind the initial plan. This plan emphasized experimental theatre enterprises in the metropolitan areas (where production groups with specialized interest might supplement and not compete with the New York stage) and demanded that the Federal Theatre should be truly national in its scope with producing centres all over the country, an integral part of community life, making use of its very limitations to work out new methods and new techniques, giving a hearing to plays by unknown dramatists with emphasis on regional and local material—a theatre alive to the passing scene, stripped of expensive ornamentation, expressing the needs, the capacities, the experience of its workers. And it must do all this, not by jeopardizing existing enterprises, but, on the contrary, by stimulating theatre interest, creating theatre audiences, and if possible making opportunity for permanent employment. Hence its emphasis on the experimental, on adventure in fields deserted by the commercial theatre, entertainment for the underprivileged, work in CCC camps, on circus, vaudeville, and variety shows for groups and localities in need of diversion and entertainment.

Never has a theatre had so many demands upon it nor had so many masters. Because it belongs to the community by right of the fact that every taxpayer willingly or unwillingly has contributed to its support, because it belongs to the Government which, theoretically at least, is the agent of the people, because it belongs to the workers who are in it, having been created to meet their desperate need, Federal Theatre is continually subjected to every possible form of pressure. It is a tremendous communal enterprise and in communal activity there is little freedom for individualistic expression. A commercial manager need only please himself and his backer. If they agree to lose money, to risk arrest or to buck public disapproval, that is their concern. When the Federal Theatre goes into production everyone, from the Secretary of State to the lady who picks up the discarded programs and turns up the seats in the deserted playhouse after the show is over, is profoundly concerned.

This vital relation between the Federal Theatre, its audience and its workers, is one of its most challenging aspects but it means that the Federal Theatre could not exist nor has it for a moment existed quietly, on the outskirts of action. It has not been able to evolve methods and techniques, try out ideas, discard failures in experimental obscurity. Everything it does is in the limelight, particularly everything it does that is new and unhallowed by custom. Its failures are among its proudest assets. What a vindication of the power of the spoken word it was—what a proof of the immense impact of the living stage as against the printed text or the shadow world of the screen—when the first Living Newspaper in America was ordered closed after the preview. No one who saw the bare stage of the Biltmore Theatre where actors in their ordinary street clothes without benefit of costume, lighting effects, make-up or properties spoke their lines—lines taken verbatim from reports, minutes of meetings and other authentic sources—will forget the moving effect of that scene. Mussolini spoke to the crowds in Rome, Haile Selassie addressed his soldiers, the 'powers' conferred at Geneva, an Ethiopian village came to life, the cities of London and Manchester were there when soap-box orators addressed the crowds. It was the same stuff of which news-reels and headlines are made, but it brought with it terror and pity. Theatrically and humanly it was dynamite. The Government, not without reason, could not take it and there were other complications, all too human, involved.

Chicago as well as New York had trouble with its opening show. *Model Tenements,* a new play by a gifted young playwright, Meyer Levin, could not open at first because the Mayor of Chicago didn't like people in tenements talking on the stage as people in tenements talk in reality (as this goes to press the difficulties seem to have been ironed out and the play is about to open). *Valley Forge,* Maxwell Anderson's noble poetic drama, could not be given in a certain town near Boston because some people thought it was disrespectful to the Father of his country and others had private feuds to attend to.

When *Triple A Plowed Under* opened, a group of war 'veterans' on the project itself demanded, without success, its immediate suppression because Earl Browder, the Communist leader, with Thomas Jefferson and other worthies, makes a brief statement to an invisible audience. And if *Ethiopia, Model Tenements, Valley Forge,* and *Triple A Plowed Under* all were subjected to varied degrees of censorship by one or another current of influence, if pro and anti anything both within and without the project causes immediate demonstration for or against with a passion of conviction that makes the welkin ring and provides the press with headline copy, then the lady of the broom becomes irate in her turn because her theatre is in danger of never opening, of being called ugly names, of failing after months of frenzied effort to produce anything at all.

With all the contending forces at work, it is not surprising that *Ethiopia* was closed but that *Triple A Plowed Under* opened and ran for weeks to capacity houses. It is not surprising that *Model Tenements* was closed but that *Chalk Dust,* which dared to comment unfavorably on certain aspects of the sacrosanct educational system of our big cities, was so successful that the Experimental Theatre had to let it run much longer than originally intended. It is not surpising that the Federal Theatre has not yet developed the new American genius but that in *Murder in The Cathedral* it has been able to give a worthy, dignified and beautiful production to an outstanding modern tragedy by an American poet.

The critical interest aroused by the experimental work of the Federal Theatre proves the soundness of the Director's continual emphasis on this phase. Experiment, however, depends on material and direction as well as on freedom of expression and both exist in insufficient quantity for a theatre the size of this one, recruited as it is from the ranks of the unemployed. There were at first only a handful of directors and theatre workers conscious of the aims and objectives of the project. This original group was enthusiastic enough to believe that while running theatre enterprises (which are always in themselves and under the most favorable circumstances slightly mad affairs) they could at the same time cope with government procedure, hold good against political pressure, handle emergency relief techniques, re-train the veterans of the theatre and guide the youngsters (whom our late lamented civilization threw into a world where there were no jobs) into new methods of expression.

All this, which at times seemed impossible, has been done and is being done in many places, though in certain areas of the country Federal Theatre, as conceived by Hallie Flanagan, has not penetrated as yet. Relief shows are going on—entertaining their tens of thousands with second-rate stock shows, but this residuum throws into relief the calibre of most of the plays given on the project: from a classic, such as *Everyman,* to a modern Pulitzer Prize play, such as *The Old Maid,* the long record reads like a 'selected list of recommended plays for various audiences.' For not only are all types of actors, good, poor or indifferent, involved in the venture, but the greatest possible variety of audiences as well, from the novelty seekers in New York who respond most eagerly to experimentation and such departures from tradition as the tropical Negro *Macbeth* in Harlem, to the small-town group who want a play they have read about in the *Times*—an *Accent on Youth* or a *Whistling in the Dark.* In all of the large centres—New York, Chicago and Los Angeles—units have been set up to put the old-timers to work on plays with which they are familiar, or which figured in American stage history: *A Texas Steer, Lightnin', Secret Service* and *Shore Acres* can once more be seen on the living stage, while Shakespeare, Goldsmith, Ibsen, Shaw and the rest are built into repertories for school, college and general consumption.

In the realm of entertainment, and of the use of special talents, the vaudeville and circus groups are among the most active, though the marionettes run them a close second. In Los Angeles the Marionette Theatre has staged *Genesis* and *The Microbe Hunters,* by way of contrast to *Puss in Boots, Pierre Patelin* and *The Crock of Gold* in San Francisco. The New York Marionettes have extensive bookings and are among the Federal Theatre's most popular actors. The making, dressing and handling of marionettes have proved a happy occupation for many older men and women who can no longer face the exigencies of appearing before the footlights. Under the experienced supervision of trained puppeteers, marionette groups are active in almost all the Federal Theatre centres, large and small, playing in schools, libraries, hospitals, asylums, homes and settlement houses and even, in Los Angeles, boasting a theatre of their own.

How far has Federal Theatre reached toward that further objective—the liberation of new creative talents in the writing field; what new playwrights has it discovered; to what fresh and vital scripts has it given life? It is too soon to answer that question. An O'Neill or an Odets does not appear every three months, and Federal Theatre has been in production less than that time. Yet it already has to its credit over a dozen new plays, one of which has been mentioned for professional production and another has been bought by the movies. In almost every unit playwriting of some sort is going forward, either in such group efforts as that employed to create the script of the Living Newspaper, to prepare material for the Texas centenary, or dramatize the history of a particular locale, or in the work of individual playwrights engaged in translating, rewriting or adapting specific plays.

Play-reading for the nation is no light matter and a play-reading section was set up in New York as one of the first units of the Federal Theatre Project. During the first months an avalanche of scripts descended upon the project, many of them war-scarred veterans of the agents' lists, others amorphous products of a misguided will to write. It was soon found that Federal Theatre had a standard of its own, and after the first flood there was a marked subsidence. It was all very well for enthusiasts on the project to maintain that they could and would produce the most difficult types of plays—poetic, experimental, topical—and produce them well. What was there to prove it? Nothing. For almost three months, nothing but difficulties, enthusiastically reported in the press, concerned with incomprehensible organization details and arguments. But when at last the turmoil and shouting died, when the house-lights in the auditorium dimmed and the footlights on the first show—with the significant title *Walk Together Chillun*—went up, a new current set in. Almost simultaneously theatres all over the country opened their doors. *The Knight of the Burning Pestle* inaugurated the educational series in California, *Jefferson Davis* toured the south, *Black Empire,* a new Negro script, was given in Los Angeles, *Brief Candle* appeared in Seattle, *Barbara Frietchie* played in its author's, Clyde Fitch's, home town, Hartford. A theatre which six months ago had no central organization, no directors, actors, scene designers, playwrights; a theatre without theatres, rehearsal rooms, executive offices or workshops; a theatre without scripts, options or production plans, operating under complications inherent in government and relief procedures, has today over three hundred and fifty shows in production and rehearsal including all the categories of Polonius, with vaudeville, variety, circus, marionette and operetta thrown in.

Many of the ills that beset the path of the Federal Theatre Project in its early days have been overcome. Requisitions are becoming child's play to the experienced directors. Weeks of intensive rehearsing and training are welding actors into competent repertory groups. Theatres are available, and, most important of all, audiences are there—audiences running into hundreds of thousands a week, in many instances new audiences, eager for the spoken word, for plays that they can afford to see. The low scale of prices is a significant factor in the situation. Teachers, workers, group leaders everywhere report the keen interest of young people who are coming, for the first time, into contact with the living theatre. With all these elements ready, the time has come to forge ahead, discard fallacious theories, build on experience and put to use the wisdom won by trial, error and success.

With the knowledge gained by its first six months of actual experience the Federal Theatre is ready to go ahead along social and constructive lines. Whether it will have this opportunity or not 'waits in the hand of God'—or of the statesmen in Washington.

29 / HOUSING IN THE SOUTH

Most of the famous Report on Economic Conditions of the South *deals with rural conditions, but the following selection shows that the South's problems were not confined to the farm.*

The effects of bad housing can be measured directly in the general welfare. It lessens industrial efficiency, encourages inferior citizenship, lowers the standard of family life, and deprives people of reasonable comfort. There are also direct relationships between poor housing and poor health, and between poor housing and crime.

The type of slum most usual in southern towns consists of antiquated, poorly built rental quarters for working people. The rows of wooden houses without any modern improvements, without proper sanitary facilities, and often without running water, are usually in congested areas and in the least desirable locations. Often they are next to mills or mines where the tenants work, or on low swampy land subject to floods and no good for anything else. They are usually far removed from playgrounds and other recreation areas. The southern slum has often been built to be a slum. It is simply a convenient barracks for a supply of cheap labor.

Lack of running water and impure water supplies are common in southern slums. Bathtubs, sinks, and laundry tubs are among the bare necessities that are often lacking in slum dwellings.

SOURCE: National Emergency Council, "Housing," *Report on Economic Conditions of the South* (Washington: United States Information Service, 1938), pp. 33–36.

Sometimes city water is supplied through a yard hydrant shared by several families. Surface wells are often contaminated on the farms and in the villages and small towns. Contaminated milk and contaminated water, frequently found, cause typhoid fever, which is becoming a widespread rural disease in the South.

Lack of sanitary flush toilets and sewer systems for waste disposal is characteristic not only of the great majority of farm and rural homes, but of a large proportion of homes in small towns and a substantial number in the cities. Twenty-six percent of southern city or town households are without indoor flush toilets as contrasted with 13.1 percent for the city and town households of the country as a whole. In extensive rural districts there are not only no indoor flush toilets, but no outdoor privies even of the most primitive sort. Nearly a fifth of all southern farm homes have no toilets at all. It is in these regions that hookworm infection and consequent anemia have flourished as a result of soil pollution.

There is also extensive overcrowding in the southern town areas. In one-eighth of the dwellings there are more than one and one-half persons per room. In the United States as a whole only one-fourteenth of town houses are so crowded. In 19 southern cities recently studied over 40 percent of all dwellings rent for less than $15 a month or are valued at less than $1,500, as opposed to 24.6 percent for the 64 cities studied in the country as a whole. Only three of the southern cities had a smaller percentage of dilapidated houses than the national average. Five of the 8 cities with over a quarter of their houses in bad condition were in the South; 1 of these had 4 out of 10 of its houses either in need of repairs or unfit for habitation.

A study of blighted areas in New Orleans showed that their tuberculosis death rate was twice as high as the city's average, that their number of criminal arrests was 40 percent higher than the average, and that syphilis and cancer rates were high.

. . . . .

If we consider below-standard all nonfarm dwellings in the 14 States renting for less than $10 a month, and all occupant-owned nonfarm dwellings valued at less than $1,500, we find 1½ million below-standard houses. Recent studies by local housing authorities in many of the southern cities indicate that these assumptions are correct. In addition, many houses now renting between $10 and $15 are definitely below standard. The average farmhouse in the South is worth about $650. The average farm renter's house is worth about $350, according to the Federal census of 1930.

Southern cities have one important advantage over northern cities in their approach to the housing problem. As a rule, they are not hampered by the excessive land valuations that have developed in the North with the rapid growth and centralization of industry. Although the 1930 census shows that the rate of movement to cities and towns is greater in the South than in the North, the effect of this is not yet reflected in town and city land values and is not likely to be while wages remain low. It is, however, reflected in poorer living conditions, overcrowding, and greater danger of the spread of certain diseases.

By the most conservative estimates, 4,000,000 southern families should be rehoused. This is one-half of all families in the South.

30 / ACROSS THE DESK OF A RELIEF ADMINISTRATOR

Excerpts from the journal of Milwaukee's relief administrator, Benjamin Glassberg, illustrate the complexities of providing assistance to the unemployed and other needy during the 1938 recession.

JANUARY 20, 1938

The 100,000th Case

On this day the Department enrolled its 100,000th case. This seemed to be a notable landmark in the onward march of the depression. It showed that since June 1, 1930, when the present numbering of case records was installed to replace the old, 100,000 cases, representing approximately 370,000 persons, have made application for relief or service. This means that close to half the population of the entire county has been sufficiently affected by the depression to feel unable to take care of themselves.

This 100,000th case is interesting in its own right. The applicant, 48 years old, is married and the father of four children, two sons and two daughters, the oldest 22 and the youngest 11. The father went to work in a shoe factory as a factory hand at 16 and was employed steadily with the same firm for thirty-one years. Early in 1937 the concern followed the migration of other shoe factories out of Milwaukee to the small towns up state, to escape dealing with the union. This left our client stranded, without a job. After he exhausted his unemployment compensation he suc-

SOURCE: Benjamin Glassberg, *Across the Desk of a Relief Administrator* (Chicago: American Public Welfare Association, 1938), pp. 19–27. Reprinted by permission.

ceeded in getting a job with a machine tool firm where his oldest son was working. He lost this job in September, when the heavy industries began their first large-scale layoffs. Two months later the son also was laid off. The father had never averaged more than $25 a week and at no time had accumulated any savings. Now he found temporary refuge in the relief rolls as number 100,000, and soon thereafter was in the ranks of the W.P.A. The *Milwaukee Sentinel* gave this story a prominent play on the first page.

. . . . .

JANUARY 21, 1938

. . . . .

How Should the Last Fifteen Dollars Be Used?

Chester MacDougall came with a letter from the supervisor of his district, who was anxious that he be interviewed. It seems that he is unemployed, having been laid off three months ago. The year before, he invested $150 in lumber and built a shack for himself and his wife. It is devoid of any conveniences, but it is home to Mr. MacDougall. But now he had exhausted all his savings, with the exception of $15, and he was concerned as to whether, before applying for relief, he could use the $15 to pay the interest on his mortgage. He feared that if he did not, he might lose his little home. He was now without food, but hesitated to do anything for fear that he might be regarded as having misused his money. A rather striking commentary of the effect of unemployment on a simple, hardworking citizen, in awe of the authorities and hesitant to do what was right and proper. He was assured that there would be no objection if he paid the interest of the mortgage and then made application for relief.

N.Y.A. Landscaping Project

Mr. John Lasher, N.Y.A. Director, visited to describe a landscaping and gardening project which is about to be developed for young boys now employed on N.Y.A. projects. The plan calls for the establishment of a resident camp for twenty-five boys in one of the county parks. The Park Commission will cooperate in the training of these boys, to help them in acquiring the art of landscaping, for which there are a number of openings both in the county park system and in greenhouses in the city. They will be given a thorough training in botany, soil erosion, and the care of plants, and will receive $25 a month while in training. Mr. Lasher was anxious to know to what extent the Department can cooperate in supplying the provisions the boys will need during the training period. He was assured that there is no question that such project is valuable and that the Department will cooperate, although it seems unnecessary to have the boys live in camps, as the plan contemplates, in view of the fact that the boys can reach the park from their homes. He felt there would be many advantages in having the boys live together during their training period.

Fan Mail

A W.P.A. worker, Frank Kwitowski, writes, making a peculiar request. He asks that he be permitted to contribute toward the support of his father-in-law's family, rather than be required to support his wife. He states that his wife deserted him and their son, and he had then gone to live with his wife's parents, where he had been living for the last seven years. He was working on the W.P.A. and his parents-in-law were receiving aid from the Outdoor Relief Department, together with $35 from Frank for payment of interest on the H.O.L.C. loan. His wife had been employed at a machine shop, averaging $100 a month. Recently she was laid off and had applied for relief. As a result he was interviewed and asked to take care of her. He pointed out that if he were to do so and also continue to pay $35 a month to his father-in-law he would not have enough for his own needs. He feels a sense of loyalty to the parents-in-law, who helped him when he was in need, and asked whether he could not be permitted to continue to aid them, instead of taking care of his wife. Investigation indicated the essential justice of Mr. Kwitowski's proposal and he was consequently permitted to continue to do just as he has been doing and his wife was granted relief.

A letter was received from Mr. M. G. East, complaining that his tenant, William Port, who is working on the W.P.A., fails to pay his rent and spends his earnings regularly on drink, adding: "We don't want to put no one out of a job. That won't help us any, but thought probably you had some method of taking care of cases of this nature when one was too weak to do for himself. His method is that he is a soldier and will always have work. They have to give him work, regardless of what they do, so will you please advise us just what to do?"

Examination of the record indicated that similar complaints concerning Mr. Port had been received previously and that his attitude was that he would not be removed from his job because he is an ex-service man. Although the Department does not attempt to act as a bill collector, it has advised clients assigned to W.P.A. jobs that they are expected to pay for their needs from their earnings, especially their rent. Failure to pay means eviction, which makes it more difficult to induce landlords to rent their premises to relief clients because of a growing fear that persons receiving public aid are not very good rent risks, in spite of the fact that the Department has been paying rent regularly throughout the depression. Since Mr. Port had been warned on a previous occasion that he would be removed from W.P.A. should he again fail to pay his rent and meet his obligations, his removal from W.P.A. was ordered.

January 24, 1938

Staff Conference; Lag in Certification; Rent for Single Persons

At the staff conference of department heads and district supervisors an effort was made to clear up the causes of the lag in certifications of clients to W.P.A. It was agreed that we should reexamine all those groups who are not being certified, to determine the correctness of the decisions previously arrived at. Discussion of this problem indicates that in many cases where the head of the household is not eligible there may be some other employable member in the family who can be certified. Since conditions in many families change rapidly, cases which may have been regarded as ineligible for certification a month or two ago may now be found to be eligible. In view of the large number of aliens who were removed from W.P.A., it is essential that they be encouraged to declare their intentions and secure their first papers. The Naturalization Project set up by the W.P.A. has agreed to visit such families, not for the purpose of an "Americanization drive" but to help with information, directions, etc. Clients are also to be encouraged to register in classes in the Social Centers. The problem of how to deal with persons receiving unemployment compensation is causing considerable concern. In view of the large number of applicants who are receiving such compensation and who are not eligible for certification to W.P.A., it is essential to keep careful check on such cases, so that certification can be effected as soon as the compensable period has come to an end.

The increasing number of applications is imposing a steadily mounting burden on the individual workers, especially in Intake and in the Visiting Districts, the case load during the last few months having risen to unusually high proportions. The only hope for improvement lies in an improvement in general industrial conditions.

The problem of the manner in which requisitions are issued for rent payments for those living in housekeeping rooms was raised by a number of supervisors. It was pointed out that landlords of housekeeping rooms are able to evict much more rapidly than renters of unfurnished rooms and therefore our procedure ought to be simplified and speeded up. At the present time, before rent is paid there must be a visit by the visitor, the landlord's signature and the rent agreement must be secured, and if it is the first rent paid for the client in question, it must be approved by the district supervisor. Before the rent is actually paid, a landlord in a housekeeping room may evict. Further discussion pointed to the fact that this does not constitute any serious problem. Where the facts indicate that the danger does exist, the case can be given early attention by the visitor in reading the record before the visit is paid and landlord agreements can be mailed promptly to the landlord for him to mail back.

A more serious phase of this problem was developed in the course of the discussion. It was pointed out that many single persons are living in two or more rooms. This is especially true of widows or widowers, who have several rooms full of furniture to which they are emotionally attached and to whom moving into a single room means parting from their possessions, which they naturally prize very highly. However, it means paying rent of $15 to $18, instead of $6 to $8, and supplying a ton of coal, as well as paying for gas and electric services, whereas, if the client were living in a single furnished room, the total cost would be cut in half at least. In view of the very heavy relief expenditures of the county, it does not seem wise to permit this to continue. There is also to be considered the housing shortage and the undesirability of maintaining a single person in a three- or four-room apartment which could be used for a family. It also appears that in many cases aged persons are unable to take care of themselves, but nevertheless cling to their furniture when they should be receiving care at the Infirmary. Such cases must be carefully studied, so that we can gradually correct these conditions.

Transient Cases

There is a constant flow of relief applicants from the southern states to the city, judging from the number of cases submitted for decision by the division dealing with nonresidents. James Parks brought his brother, Moses, who had been living in Mississippi, as well as his mother, Mary, who had been living in Arkansas, to Milwaukee in June 1937. James was working at the time, but shortly thereafter he was laid off and he was unable to continue supporting his mother and brother, or himself. They had now applied for relief, misrepresenting the time of their arrival in the county. Investigation established the place of their legal settlement and permission was granted by both states for the return of Moses and Mrs. Parks. In the meantime relief was granted to Mrs. Parks and Moses, as well as extensive medical care, including hospitalization from time to time, for Moses was suffering from a syphilitic condition which required careful treatment. During the greater part of his stay to date Moses has been in the County Hospital. However, the physicians stated that he was ready for discharge and would not require the services of a physician for a long period and, therefore, was able to travel alone. However, both he and his mother refuse to return, stating with some justice that they would probably not be given relief in the place of their legal settlement. James insists that Milwaukee County must continue to give them relief and that there is no law which makes it necessary for them to leave Milwaukee.

Since the place where each had legal settlement acknowledges responsibility, it was felt that they would have to return, and it was decided to discontinue relief. In view of the complete absence of any federal reimbursement for relief and the almost negligible assistance granted through the State Public Welfare Department, there seems no alternative but to refuse aid to nonresidents who can be returned to their place of legal settlement.

In another case calling for consideration it appeared that Joseph Daniels had left Milwaukee County in 1935 and had moved with his family to White River Township, North Dakota, where he had an opportunity to farm on land owned by a relative. This was done with the approval of the township authorities. The Department helped furnish transportation to White River. In April 1937 Mr. Daniels returned to Milwaukee with his family. He had been absent for over a year and had lost legal settlement in Milwaukee and established it in White River. For three months he was employed in a machine shop and when laid off applied for relief. Correspondence with North Dakota and the officers of White River Township definitely disclosed that Mr. Daniels and his family had acquired legal settlement in that township, but the town officers refused to acknowledge this and threatened to return the family if arrangements were made to return them to North Dakota. Apparently this was done on the theory that Daniels' family had spent most of their lives in Milwaukee and should be accepted.

In view of the very technical position assumed by other relief departments and the fact that Milwaukee, because of the somewhat more liberal attitude displayed in assuming not only its legal, but frequently its moral responsibility, is usually doing more than its share, it was decided to discontinue relief to the Daniels family and to insist upon their availing themselves of their right to return to White River Township. In this case there is no justification for White River's refusing to assume responsibility for a family which has clearly acquired settlement.

JANUARY 25, 1938

Refusal to Accept Assignment to W.P.A.

Although it is occasionally necessary to recommend the removal of a worker from W.P.A. because earnings are spent on drink, there are on the other hand occasionally clients who refuse to accept W.P.A. assignments. The problem presented in such cases is a serious one. To deny aid to such a family means punishing a wife and children, as well as the person refusing the job. Throughout all previous work programs no attempt at compulsion was resorted to in such cases and the principle of voluntary labor was adhered to. Since there never were as many jobs as were demanded by persons on relief, there was no special point in insisting on an unwilling worker's accepting a job. However, now that the W.P.A. quota has been greatly increased and there is room for all those technically employable, it seems unfair to carry anyone on direct relief who can be cared for through federal funds. The problem was finally submitted to the Board of Trustees, who ruled that the head of the house refusing a job should be denied relief, but relief can continue to be made available for the family. While this is not an altogether satisfactory solution of the problem, it is more reasonable than cutting off the family entirely. The application of the rule is to be restricted to such cases as are directly discussed with the Superintendent, however. A case in point was presented today:

Mr. John Petersen had come to Milwaukee from South Dakota in a trailer. He borrowed some furniture from relatives in Milwaukee and established himself here. He had worked in Milwaukee from 1928 to 1930, had returned to South Dakota in that year, and came back in 1933. He was granted relief and assigned to an F.E.R.A. project in August 1934. He was removed, however, because he refused to have a physical examination. He then received relief until the W.P.A. program was established and in November 1935 he was offered a W.P.A. job, which he refused because it was too far from home. The following month he refused again on the ground that he was not a common laborer, but a mason, although there was nothing in his work history to indicate that. Shortly thereafter he was sent to Washington by the Workers' Alliance to participate in their demonstration for an enlarged W.P.A. program. (This attitude was in no sense typical of Workers' Alliance members.) When advised to get some additional furniture for his family, such as beds, stoves and chairs, which he could earn by working at the Goodwill, he refused. In November 1936 he was finally assigned as a mason, earning $90 a month. He worked two months and was laid off and has been receiving relief since. He has steadily refused reassignments to W.P.A. since that time. In view of the fact that there are no health reasons which would explain refusal to accept W.P.A. work, he was informed that the rule recently adopted by the Board of Trustees would make it necessary for the Department to remove him from the family relief code. He continued in his refusal to accept work, stating that he would never work as a laborer, although he could produce no verification of any work history as a skilled worker. If necessary he would leave the county and find work elsewhere. He has no plans and does not feel that his wife will express any concern if he does leave.

Problem of Dental Care

The lack of sufficient provision for dental care was the subject of a conference with the Manager of County Institutions, Juvenile Court Judge, and representatives of other county welfare agencies and institutions. It was pointed out that a good many of the children brought before the Juvenile Court charged with delinquency are found to be, on examination, suffering from some physical ailment and that practically all are badly in need of dental care. The Chief Probation Officer feels that this is a very serious problem; that many a girl who feels that her appearance is marred by bad teeth will do many things to attract the attention which she can not get normally because of her appearance. The Judge of the Juvenile Court also pointed out that many of the mothers' pension families are badly in need of medical and dental care and that it would be advisable to make available the physicians' and dentists' services which relief families are getting. It was agreed that this matter required further attention and another meeting will be called within the near future to outline a plan.

31 / THE CITIES TAKE POLITICAL POWER

When the noted political pollster, Samuel Lubell, set out in 1940, to discover how Franklin D. Roosevelt had been able to win an unprecedented third term, he found the answer in the cities.

Much more than the third-term tradition was shattered when President Roosevelt took the oath of office again on Monday.

Who elected him? As in all elections, there were many cross-currents, but the 1940 answer is simple and inescapable.

The little fellow elected him, because there are more of the little fellow and because he believed Mr. Roosevelt to be his friend and protector.

Roosevelt won by the vote of Labor, unorganized as well as organized, plus that of the foreign born and their first and second generation descendants. And the Negro.

It was a class-conscious vote for the first time in American

SOURCE: Samuel Lubell, "Postmortem: Who Elected Roosevelt?" *Saturday Evening Post,* CCXIII (January 25, 1941), 9–11, 91–96.

history, and the implications are portentous. The New Deal appears to have accomplished what the Socialists, the I. W. W. and the Communists never could approach. It has drawn a class line across the face of American politics. That line seems to be there to stay. While thousands of wage earners, even voters on relief, voted for Willkie, we are talking here about groups as wholes.

Mr. Roosevelt is the first President to owe his election in such great measure to the teeming cities. On the farms and in the towns Mr. Willkie more than held his own. It was in the industrial centers that the Republican hopes were blacked out in factory smoke.

The Republican campaign had virtually no effect on this vote, the evidence argues. I doubt that anything Willkie might have done would have affected it. The election was not decided on the issues he debated, but on forces long at work—economic status, nationalities, birth rates. The rise of Government as an employer on a scale rivaling the biggest business is a fourth. And the indications are that this vote might have gone to Roosevelt for a fourth or a fifth term as readily as for a third.

. . . The Republicans do not know what hit them; the Democrats, certainly as distinguished from the New Dealers, do not know what they hit the Republicans with. The New Deal has aimed at a bloodless revolution.

In 1940 it went a long way toward accomplishing it.

In numbers it was no great victory. Roosevelt won by the smallest plurality and the smallest percentage of the total vote since the neck-and-neck election of 1916. If his strength should diminish between now and 1944 at the same rate it did between 1936 and 1940, he would be beaten in 1944.

The opposition is taking comfort in these figures, but the 1940 vote upset the fundamentals of our old two-party system, and when the fundamentals are overturned, past-performance figures are worthless.

In considerable measure the vote was personal for Mr. Roosevelt. No one may say how far, if he does not run for a fourth term, he might be able to deliver this vote in 1944 to an heir.

What is clear is that, once Roosevelt is out of the picture, this vote will not slip back automatically into its former slots. The political wars henceforth will be fought with new tactics and new weapons to unpredictable results.

I say this on the basis of a firsthand study of thirteen of the cities, from Boston to Seattle, which piled up the Roosevelt vote. While the body still was warm, the Post sent me to hold a post-mortem.

. . . . .

Boston

In the shadow of the Bunker Hill Monument, in historic Charlestown, Roosevelt rolled up a plurality of nearly four to one. The frame houses built in the days of Edward Everett still stand. Mounting the narrow hillside streets to the monument, they seem heaped one on top of another in factory-district congestion, the back yards barely providing clothesline space. Living in those homes today are longshoremen, foundry workers, packers, waitresses and minor city employees. About 65 per cent are Irish Catholic.

A typical Boston working-class district, Charlestown is not a slum. Poorer sections of the city went nine to one for Roosevelt. Prevailing incomes of Charlestown families range from $1200 to $1500; about one in five own their homes. Those who do are mighty proud of it. Good-sized metal plates proclaiming the owner's name are nailed to every door like family shields.

William J. Galvin, the thirty-six-year-old councilman and Democratic ward leader, has a simple explanation for the Roosevelt vote: "Probably no section in the country gained more under the New Deal." Galvin can check off the gains against the total ward population of 30,000: Hundreds got pay raises under the wage-hour law; more hundreds of seasonal workers are having slack months cushioned by unemployment-insurance benefits. The NYA is helping from 300 to 500 youths; at the worst of the depression thousands held WPA jobs; of 1500 persons past sixty-five in the ward, more than 600 receive old-age assistance; another 600 cases are on direct relief and get aid for dependent children. Charlestown is a food-stamp area; the WPA improved its bathing beach; a new low-cost housing project will relieve some of the ward's congestion.

. . . . .

To Charlestown's Irish, the New Deal has meant an advance along other fronts too. They are the sons and daughters, the grandsons and granddaughters of the immigrants who swarmed into Boston in the last quarter of the nineteenth century. Then the "Yankee vote" ruled Massachusetts. Classified-job advertisements carried notices, "No Irish need apply."

But the immigrant Irish reared larger families than the Yankees. Through sheer numbers, they toppled the barriers in profession after profession. By the 20's they had acquired local political dominance. Being Democrats under Republican Presidents, though, they were denied Federal recognition until Roosevelt.

Reporters in the Boston Federal Building cannot recall a single Irishman on the U. S. district court before 1933. Roosevelt has made two appointments to that court, the names, Sweeney and Ford. Postmaster Peter Tague, who lives in Charlestown, is Irish, as are the collector of customs, the U. S. marshal, several assistant U. S. attorneys. In Charlestown alone, Galvin estimates, Irishmen have got more than 400 Federal jobs under the New Deal. Not only for the poor but for those better off economically, Roosevelt has become the champion of the Irish climb up the American ladder.

. . . . .

MILWAUKEE

. . . Milwaukee, with its huge population of German descent, was figured to give the President only a slight lead. When the returns were in, Roosevelt had the surprising plurality of more than 70,000. While the Poles, the second largest nationality group in the city, contributed heavily, the decisive factor was the shift of the Socialists, who control half the city council.

In the seventh ward, Alderman Alex Ruffing, Socialist, has been elected and re-elected since 1918 almost invariably by a two-to-one margin. Last November, Roosevelt got 6860 votes in the ward to Willkie's 3470. Norman Thomas crumb-picked 504 votes. Normally, Thomas can count on 50,000 votes in all Milwaukee. In 1940 he got 11,000. Stack that 39,000 difference against the 25,000 or so votes by which Roosevelt carried Wisconsin.

The seventh ward's Socialists are not the radical type. They are about evenly split between native and foreign born, with about 70 per cent of German Protestant extraction. Their Socialism was inherited from their ancestors who fled from Germany in 1848. Of middle-class means, their rentals average around thirty dollars a month. About 40 per cent own their homes, which range in value from $2000 to $7000.

Mostly the workers are skilled artisans—mechanics, bricklayers, carpenters and shoe workers. At the depression's worst, one half of them were unemployed; Ruffing would have 150 and more job-seeking callers a day. In recent months the indigent callers have dwindled to three or four a week.

The Socialist shift to Roosevelt, Ruffing explains with a little shrug of inevitability: "He enacted all the laws we Socialists had advocated for years."

The very closeness of the vote in Wisconsin seems to have swelled the Roosevelt outpouring. In keeping with German tradition that a woman's place is in the kitchen, many seventh-ward women had never exercised their voting right. In November they hung that tradition up with their aprons and swarmed to the polls, lest Roosevelt's social reforms be lost.

Detroit

Roosevelt's greatest pluralities in Wayne County were registered in the Polish districts of Hamtramck, where precincts went twenty and thirty to one for him. More typical of the city as a whole, though, are two auto-worker precincts in the twenty-first ward which went for Roosevelt three to one.

Economically, these precincts fall into the great average sectors of Detroit. They are a food-stamp area; incomes run between $1200 and $1400 a year; neighborhood movies charge twenty cents admission; the well-kept private homes are worth between $2500 and $5000. "Sleeping room for rent" signs in many windows mirror the transient, half-boom, half-broke nature of auto-plant employment.

Workers in the two precincts are predominantly native white, better than half Protestant. In a random apartment house one finds such names as Baldwin, Walsh, Gibson, Calhoun, Costello, Powers, Snyder, Saltzgiver and Solomon. Perhaps a fourth of the workers came up from the South during the 20's. Labor says that these "hillbillies," as they are known, were brought in because it was felt that they would be less inclined to join unions and would be easier to handle. Today the hillbillies are high in union councils.

Chrysler Local Seven, in the fore of the sit-down strike of 1937, has its headquarters in one precinct. The local has its own three-floor building, which at shift time becomes a buzz of activity. Four girls behind teller windows collect dues—the local claims 10,000 members. A stream of visitors pours in and out of the offices of the president and the shop committee.

Nearly fifty such United Auto Workers locals are scattered throughout the city. Their listings in the telephone book run to half a column. Only the state, Federal and municipal governments have longer listings. Like many another union, the UAW has become a big business, with its own white-collar opportunities. A stenographer working at Chrysler Seven is the daughter of an auto worker; the educational director is a young man in his thirties, fresh out of the plant. He still wears a work shirt and lumber jacket, but he sits at a desk with a telephone and a buzzer.

Even more so than with the Irish in Boston, Roosevelt, to these auto workers, is the "friend" who gave them recognition. The New Deal enabled them to build their union. It taught them the strength of their numbers, and with the feeling of power has come a growing class-consciousness. The workers themselves use the phrase. "I'm franker than you," one local official replied when I asked him why he voted for Roosevelt. "I'll say it, even though it doesn't sound nice. We've grown class-conscious."

. . . . .

Los Angeles

Even where organized labor still is battling for a foothold, Roosevelt's appeal to the workingman proved overwhelming. Los Angeles has long been known as "open shop." In 1928 Hoover carried the city's fifth district handily; Roosevelt swept it by three to one in 1940.

The skilled craftsmen in the metal and building trades who live here belong to the AFL. The great mass of unskilled and semiskilled workers remain unorganized, although the CIO is winning adherents. Two rubber factories are located near the district; in one the United Rubber Workers have a contract. A near-by steel mill has signed with the CIO.

Save for a few apartment houses the district is composed of small homes, mainly frame bungalows. About 40 per cent are owned by the workers; rents for the others run from twenty to thirty dollars. Rents are low in Los Angeles, and this area falls in the middle third for the city. About one fourth of the families earn less than $1800; the others up to $2500.

Minneapolis

"Traditionally Republican" is the political label still applied to both Minneapolis and Minnesota. In 1938 youthful Harold Stassen broke the Farmer-Labor hold. In 1940, political experts reasoned, the pendulum would continue its swing back to "normal" Republicanism. To their surprise, Roosevelt carried the city by 17,000, the state by 47,000. What happened to the pendulum?

As in every city sampled, Minneapolis' vote broke primarily along economic lines. In the seven lowest-income wards, with rentals averaging under thirty dollars a month, Roosevelt won by better than two and a half to one. In the four wards with rentals from thirty to forty dollars a month, it was Roosevelt by seven to six. In the three wards where the rental average topped forty dollars, Willkie won by five to three. Roosevelt managed to squeeze through in one of these three wards by 8251 to 8066. In the highest-income ward, Willkie's margin fell just under three to one.

One ward which helped check the pendulum's swing was the tenth, where the late Floyd Olson, the Farmer-Labor leader, lived. A newer residential district lying near the north end of town, the ward scales about halfway on Minneapolis' economic ladder. It scores seventh in relief cases; average in department-store deliveries; better than average in automobiles owned.

In the precinct sampled, where Roosevelt led by two to one, virtually all the families own their homes. Mainly frame-and-stucco dwellings with sun-parlor porches, they fall into the FHA value range, from $4000 to $7000. Most incomes run between $1800 and $2500, with a goodly number of workers earning better than $3000.

High-school education for the children is about universal; college rare. Roughly 70 per cent are of Norwegian or Swedish descent, the dominant nationalities in the city. Sympathy for Norway helped Roosevelt.

Minneapolis is an AFL union city and probably 80 per cent of the workers in the precinct are unionized. Major occupations are the metal and building trades, trucking and driving milk wagons. Truckers and milk drivers belong to the Teamsters Union, which is popularly credited with running City Hall.

Roosevelt made his first campaign speech before the Teamsters Convention in Washington, reminding the union of its progress in membership under the New Deal, from 70,000 to 400,000. The Teamsters needed little reminding. Like the railroaders, they went down the line for their "friend" in the White House. The head of one precinct church with a number of teamsters in his congregation was outspoken in condemning the third term. He admitted bitterly, "I don't suppose I changed a single vote."

. . . . .

Seattle

. . . The Upper Broadway district here is an old, settled neighborhood. Its population is almost exclusively native white. In 1928 it went Hoover two to one; in 1940 Roosevelt by three to two.

. . . It is not a deeply rooted area of family residences. Once the fashionable part of the city, it now is being passed over for the automobile reaches near Lake Washington and the bluff overlooking Puget Sound. Many an old private residence has been converted into a duplex or a rooming house. In the last twenty years a number of medium-priced apartment houses have been erected. Rents average from thirty dollars to forty-five dollars a month.

White-collar workers predominate. An afternoon's interviewing yielded a municipal-transit employee, a telephone installer, a salesman, druggist, insurance agent, office manager, longshoreman, real-estate man, teacher, bookkeeper, cashier and chemist. Their incomes ran from $1500 to $2200 a year. The shops in the neighborhood, one and two stories high, fit typical middle-class needs—groceries, bakeries, hamburger spots, restaurants, filling stations, cabinetmakers, tailors. Some storekeepers live over their shops.

Pittsburgh

As our samples mount the economic ladder, Roosevelt's margin of victory drops off. Two striking features about this "economic voting" stand out. First, wards and precincts falling into the same economic strata yield virtually the same results; there are almost no freak reversals. So sharp is the cleavage that the campaign could hardly have changed any appreciable number of votes. If the election was close in the total popular vote cast, it also was peculiarly decisive in that there seems to have been little wavering between economic groups.

The second striking feature is that in city after city the dividing line, where the great Roosevelt pluralities dwindle to a close squeeze and finally merge into slight leads for Willkie, falls across roughly the same incomes.

In Pittsburgh, Roosevelt got nearly 75 per cent of the vote in wards with average rentals below forty dollars a month. In the highest-income districts, with rentals of sixty-five dollars and better, he received only 40 per cent of the vote. Somewhere between the forty-five and sixty dollar rentals the New Deal edge broke.

In Cleveland one has to go into the suburbs to find a district at that income level; Roosevelt carried every ward in the city. In Minneapolis, with stronger Republican traditions and a goodly population of German descent, the break for Willkie came in a ward which averages forty-four dollars a month.

In Milwaukee three wards fall between forty and fifty dollars. Roosevelt squeezed through in two by 5868 to 5573 and 6621 to 6546, Willkie carried the third by 5245 to 4747. Willkie also won Milwaukee's only plus-sixty-dollar rental ward.

. . . . .

Harlem

How great has been the impact of this urban revolt upon the traditional Republican line-up can be seen in the Negro vote. Only in St. Louis, which continues to draw them from the South, do the Negroes still seem divided in their allegiances between the party of Lincoln and the party of Roosevelt. Harlem's Seventeenth Assembly District went better than seven to one for the New Deal.

Probably 50 per cent of Harlem's Negroes are getting relief of some kind. Older Negroes—they're most likely to be Republican—shake their graying heads ruefully and mutter, "Our people are selling their birthrights for a mess of pottage."

To the younger Negroes the WPA and relief mean not only material aid but a guaranty that no longer must they work at any salary given them, that they are entitled—they emphasize the word—to a living wage. Through the WPA, Harlem's Negroes have had opened to them white-collar opportunities which before had been shut, such as the music and art and writers' projects. Negroes, too, remember that Mrs. Roosevelt visited Harlem personally, that President Roosevelt has appointed more Negroes to administrative positions paying around $5000 a year than any President before him. Each time Roosevelt makes such an appointment, the Amsterdam News, Harlem's leading newspaper, headlines it in 72-point type. Every young Negro gets a vicarious thrill thinking, "There may be a chance up there for me."

Harlem definitely has grown class as well as race conscious. Last year the Seventeenth for the first time got a Negro installed as Democratic leader of the district. Under the warming hand of the great white father in Washington a flock of unions has sprung up. They include garment workers, janitors, bartenders, waitresses, waiters, Pullman porters, laundry workers, newspapermen, retail clerks and redcaps.

Consumer and tenant leagues have arisen to battle with Harlem's disgraceful housing problem. All sorts of groups are pressing campaigns to force neighborhood stores, once manned entirely by whites, to hire Negroes. . . .

Today, Negroes work in hundreds of establishments as behind-the-counter salesmen, as movie cashiers, as meat cutters, as salesgirls in department stores. Some labor groups hold daily classes to teach Negroes selling, typing and stenography. This is done so that the unions will be able to rebuff employers who protest, "I can't hire Negroes; they're not experienced." The proportion of Negro-owned stores is growing.

Whether or not Roosevelt is responsible, he gets the credit. In many a Harlem home hangs a rotogravure photograph of the new emancipator; some families have spent fifty cents to have it framed.

A young police reporter on the News summed it up when he remarked, "Negroes feel Roosevelt started something."

"Something" certainly has been started. In 1932 Roosevelt became President in a popular recoil against the depression. His third-term victory, however, is the result of an upsurging of the urban masses. In the New Deal they have found their leveling philosophy; under it they have been given recognition through patronage, benefits and new opportunities; they have been awakened to the consciousness of the power of their numbers.

From the GOP viewpoint, the harshest fact this post-mortem reveals is that the Republicans are on the wrong side of the birth rate, not so much the current rate as the birth rates of 1890, 1900, 1910 and 1920, which are beyond their rectifying. Grade-school enrollments have begun to fall, but not high-school enrollments as yet. For another two or three presidential elections the elements which re-elected Roosevelt will continue to grow in voting strength, actually and relatively.

Thus far, these elements are united behind Roosevelt personally. Can the Democratic Party hold them, apart from Roosevelt? If it can, then it may become the normal majority party, with the Republicans occupying the unenviable position of the Democrats after the Civil War. . . .

PART VI

The Metropolitan Society

WITH the outbreak of World War II, the Great Depression and the innovations of the New Deal came to an end. Relief programs were discontinued as jobs became plentiful. The end of the fighting brought, instead of the feared return of depression, an unprecedented boom. The effects of this prosperity on the cities was cataclysmic. Business expanded beyond the old central core and millions of Americans moved to suburbia and exurbia in search of small town values in an essentially urban setting (Selection 32). The flight of business and population from the city proper, coupled with enforced neglect during the depression years, turned the old downtown areas into shabby vestiges of their former glory. Spurred by federal urban renewal funds and local initiative some cities developed bold and imaginative plans for revival of their centers (Selection 33).

The most alarming urban development of the postwar years was the steady growth and physical and social deterioration of the Negro ghettoes. Southern Negroes, fleeing the anachronistic rural society of Dixie, found Harlem and its counterparts in other cities a dubious exchange (Selection 34).

The pervading problem of the cities, despite grand ideas and fatuous hopes, was unplanned change or none at all. Sheer ugliness was becoming institutionalized, quality was almost atavistic. Here and there, however, a voice was heard calling for the preservation of what was good and for excellence in what was being newly built (Selection 35).

At last, in the mid-1960's, it appeared that the United States had accepted the cities where nearly three-fourths of the population now lived. Pressed by President Johnson, the Congress had finally approved the cabinet-rank equality of the city with the farm (Selection 36).

32 / DECENTRALIZATION IN MEGALOPOLIS

A detailed and scholarly study of the Los Angeles area, the most notorious example of metropolitan sprawl, by political scientists Winston W. Crouch and Beatrice Dinerman, shows the persistence of old attitudes of localism and the birth of new ones.

Voluntary organizations with community orientation pervade every section of the Los Angeles metropolitan area. If one can visualize a map of the county denoting the location of each chamber of commerce, coördinating council, and related service organization, one would see a distinct clustering of such community associations within the numerous local, place-name areas that comprise this political entity. Virtually every local-name community in the county, irrespective of legal boundary lines, has, within its border, an independent community coördinating council, chamber of commerce, Kiwanis Club, Rotary, or similar voluntary organization.

Most organizations of this type are established in response to a felt need, on the part of their leaders, for programs aimed at

SOURCE: Winston W. Crouch and Beatrice Dinerman, *Southern California Metropolis: A Study in Development of Government for a Metropolitan Area* (Berkeley and Los Angeles: University of California Press, 1963), pp. 278–85. Reprinted by permission.

community betterment. In almost every case, the leaders define problems and issues in terms of the place-name area which the association is designed to serve. In a large number of cases, the organization has been established for the express purpose of strengthening community identification by providing the designated area with a representative body that would focus its attention exclusively upon problems and requirements of the limited geographic environment. A number of areas formerly affiliated with associations in adjacent communities have subsequently dissolved their relationship with the parent body and formed their own associations, with a view to asserting their separate area identities. Once established, organizational programs focus upon activities that are expected to achieve a greater amount of local improvements; the community serves as the matrix from which a majority of the organization's functions and projects emanate.

The internal structure of most community organizations, which generally includes an elected executive board and a number of special committees, follows a common pattern and is of no special significance in itself. The important feature is the type of individual responsible for performing managerial functions. Most of those serving in an executive capacity, that is, as officers or as members of the governing board, are either residents or businessmen in the community served by the organization. The governing bodies of community organizations are therefore composed of individuals who are motivated by a highly personalized concern for the future of their respective locality. Members, as well as the leadership, are drawn from a localized area, with a majority of the total composed of residents or businessmen closely associated with community affairs.

It is interesting to note that each community organization is characterized by fairly well-defined jurisdictional boundaries, despite the absence of any formal procedure for delimiting their respective spheres of influence. The coverage of each association is arrived at almost automatically and without formal or informal discussions with leaders of adjacent community organizations. Yet incidents of jurisdictional disputes among two or more like organizations claiming jurisdiction over the same geographical area are rare. Similarly, overlapping membership rarely occurs. Two adjoining chambers of commerce seldom draw their membership from the same streets, and, in many cases, membership areas of one chamber are separated from those of a neighboring organization by several noncommercial blocks from which neither draws any members. The satisfactory operation of numerous adjoining community organizations, in the absence of any prior formal agreement, would seem to reflect the presence of community areas that are psychologically separate, despite an ecological cohesiveness and, in many cases, a legal unity. An individual tends to gravitate toward the particular community with which he identifies his interests most closely. This attitude will determine his decision to affiliate with one organization, as opposed to an identical type located in an adjoining community. From a technical point of view, lines that separate community organizations from one another are arrived at arbitrarily, in the sense that they are not products of any objective analysis, are often not explicitly stated, and are determined and perpetuated without formal decision-making. Yet organizational boundary lines manifest a highly rational pattern, in that they reflect a community of interests bound together by problems and characteristics associated with fairly specific geographical areas.

Is there a relationship between the intensity of an individual's loyalty to a particular area and the size of that area? Or, expressed another way, is there a geographical limit beyond which close personal identification and loyalty cannot be achieved? An individual might well experience a considerable degree of difficulty in identifying his own personal welfare with the concerns of too broad a geographical area. Affairs of the smaller community in which the same individual resides, having a more direct impact upon his personal welfare, are clearly felt and easily recognized. An individual may experience a strong sense of personal involvement over a situation of gang warfare in close proximity to his residence or place of business, which he could not possibly experience when problems of juvenile delinquency are presented to him within the framework of a broader region.

In the latter instance, personal repercussions are indirect, at best, and the individual's reaction could not possibly be as intense. This may explain the rationale behind the existence of numerous independent organizations performing identical functions within the municipal boundaries of Los Angeles, while another municipality such as Culver City, for example, is adequately served by a much smaller number of organizations covering the entire municipality. It would seem that residents of Culver City are psychologically capable of recognizing an areawide community of interests within an area of eight square miles. Apparently, this same type of loyalty and identification cannot be realized by the inhabitants of the city of Los Angeles, scattered over an area of 457 square miles.

The concept of the community is based upon the assumption that each community possesses certain characteristics that serve to distinguish it from adjoining territory; a "personality" that is somehow different from that of neighboring areas. That these distinctions do, in fact, exist is illustrated by the degree to which special traits associated with certain areas affect the operation of community coördinating councils serving those areas. Observations regarding the manner in which council representatives interpret the nature of their communities apply, in large part, to other local organizations.

Why are certain areas more community-oriented than others? Are there certain essential ingredients present in community-minded areas that are lacking in others?

Community coördinating councils, a relatively widespread form of social organization, have a twofold purpose. First, they seek to stimulate active "grass-roots" participation in community affairs by serving as forums through which residents are encouraged to offer viewpoints and suggestions regarding local problems. Second, being composed largely of representatives from preëxisting local organizations, they attempt to unify the efforts of numerous independent associations operating at the community level.

The growth and development of coördinating councils throughout Los Angeles County is facilitated and encouraged by the Los Angeles County Department of Community Services. The entire county is divided into eleven administrative regions, and each region is served by an area consultant servicing approximately eight to ten councils. The consultant, operating in an advisory capacity, helps to organize and develop councils by coördinating the work of the several private and public agencies, committees, and organizations that seek to strengthen community life in each area.

The Department of Community Services has developed its own criteria for identifying a community, for the purpose of determining an optimum base on which to form a coördinating council. These include specific ecological, geographical, and psychological aspects (for example, does the individual recognize it as a community?). Political identification, the sharing of certain important institutions (for example, transportation, newspapers, schools, police, markets, recreation, parks, public service), and common community problems are also included. Community characteristics deemed essential to successful council operation include a reasonably stable population, a substantial segment of community population affiliated with some type of community organization, a strong leadership corps, and a community attitude favorable to the acceptance of assistance. The degree to which these ingredients exist in any given area will, according to the department, determine the degree of community consciousness inherent in the area and the relative success or failure of council operations.

. . . . .

The concept of localism, a permanent feature of our political tradition, is reflected in adverse reactions toward any proposed system that smacks of centralization or seeks to increase further the size of what is already deemed to be "big government." It is charged that a metropolitan government would be unwieldy and unresponsive. Public officials would be far removed from the citizens they are designed to serve. Services provided by a single centralized agency remote from the scene of day-to-day performance would inevitably fall short of local requirements. Politically, these sentiments tend to obviate the possibility of transferring *all* substantive local powers to a metropolitan-wide authority. When a metropolitan government is discussed, it is generally done so in terms of a *federated* system based upon a federation of existing local units coördinated under a single authority with jurisdiction over matters of regional interest. Existing local units would continue as they now are in relation to their local functions; only the metropolitan aspects of certain functions would come under the jurisdiction of the metropolitan authority. Local sentiments and authority are thereby preserved through a retention of power over matters deemed to be of a purely local nature. Yet, even these proposals would require local units to relinquish power and responsibility over certain functions that formerly fell within their province.

. . . . .

Community consciousness finds expression, sometimes, in extreme forms of behavior that approach the ridiculous. An excellent example of community pride thwarting a rational program is afforded by an effort on the part of Los Angeles City officials to implement a program of uniform community signs for the San Fernando Valley. This program was initially recommended by the city Traffic Department to help reduce the uncertainty of driving in unfamiliar areas by identifying all established communities by means of uniform markers. Place-name definition is essential to adequate city planning, traffic control, civil defense, statistical surveys, marketing, and merchandising. Nevertheless, implementation of this relatively simple program has been delayed for two years because Valley residents have been unable to agree on the precise boundaries separating their respective communities. It was announced, at the outset, that the city government would refrain from dictating the boundary locations of Valley communities, that the Valley residents themselves would make the decisions. Although there is widespread "theoretical" approval of this sign program, conflicting territorial demands have prevented its implementation.

Institutional decentralization, by providing the amenities of both urban and suburban living to the residents of Greater Los Angeles, seemingly produced an atmosphere of complacency that is incompatible with demand for comprehensive changes in the machinery of local government. This situation is exemplified by the community chamber of commerce point of view toward governmental change. A recent study . . . revealed that 54 per cent of the chamber managers noted weaknesses in the present governmental system but were anxious to work for improvements; 23 per cent were favorable to establishing a metropolitan authority; and 22 per cent were strongly in favor of existing arrangements. In other words, a proposed radical revision, such as a metropolitan-wide authority, would probably face opposition by three-fourths of the local chamber leadership. The major reasons given in justifying the viewpoints are even more revealing. They included fear of losing local autonomy and home rule, belief that "big government" generally is dangerous, and uncertainty as to whether a centralized governmental structure would provide adequate attention to community needs. Those favoring revisions were disturbed chiefly by existing deficiencies in local legislative bodies and poor legislative understanding of community needs. Little reference was made by any of those interviewed to positive advantages that might accrue to the metropolitan area through areawide administration and control.

. . . . .

33 / DOWNTOWN REVIVAL

The mayors of three cities, two of them among the nation's oldest and one in the center of the fastest growing state, tell how they met the problems of decaying downtown areas.

Statement by James H. J. Tate, Mayor of Philadelphia

Historically, the American city is a remarkable product of a dynamic country. It is a symbol of national vitality which, like a human being, has changed and grown with the passing of the years. In humans, growth and change are accepted as normal, but because we know so much about ourselves and so little about our cities, these same forces of change and growth in urban centers have too often led to pessimistic speculation about the future.

Change is frequently confused with decay. Congestion is equated with civil disaster. The growth of the suburbs is carelessly described as a flight from the city.

None of this pessimism is valid. The American city, with all its faults and shortcomings, is one of the great phenomena of American civilization.

This is not to say that problems do not exist, or that we can wait for solutions from future generations. All of us are in a daily race with time to renew and to rebuild, but we must recognize that composed as it is of bricks and mortar, macadam and structural steel, the city never quite catches up with itself. As a

SOURCE: "Workshop: Renewing Downtown," *City Problems of 1964: Proceedings, 1964 Annual Conference, United States Conference of Mayors*, ed. Wilbur H. Baldinger (Washington: United States Conference of Mayors, 1964), pp. 14–22.

living organism, it is constantly shedding its own skin and, more slowly, growing a new one.

The physical and literal heart of the city is its central area. Here, whether described as downtown, uptown, the Loop, or merely as center city, the great forces of commerce are concentrated in banks, department stores and shops. The forces of industry are channeled through headquarters in office buildings. The professions, education, vast cultural resources, research and medical centers—all the very reasons for the existence of the city—are to be found. What happens downtown affects every citizen intimately. Here the city is governed—here the entire package is put together and made to work. Just as blood flows through the human heart, so the life blood of the city flows through the downtown district.

In my own City of Philadelphia, more than one million people travel downtown daily to work, shop, learn, eat or be entertained. Increasing numbers are coming downtown to live in townhouses and apartments. Philadelphia is a city of two million, and it stands in the center of a region of four and one-half million people, encompassing eight counties in two states.

In order to keep this heart pumping productively, about $100 million of federal and city direct renewal funds provided the necessary seed money for renewal work which is now under way to the tune of $1.5 billion.

Decisions are being made every day by businessmen who are responsible for locating millions of dollars of capital investment. Whether these go to strengthen center city or are disbursed throughout the region and beyond will depend on the practical fact of the richness of the physical facilities of downtown. It will depend also on the type of symbol downtown represents in the minds of the people who live in the region.

All of our planning has been based on the initiative potential of the private enterprise system. Government activity is restricted to the absolute minimum necessary to provide a framework which stimulates the imagination of private investors and which includes the facilities necessary to support those investments after they are made.

Penn Center, Philadelphia's most famous renewal landmark, was made possible by the removal of the old Chinese Wall and the Pennsylvania Railroad tracks. It came about with government guidance and encouragement but was financed solely by private enterprise. Today, this project alone accounts for over $125 million of private capital investment. Commenting recently, the President of the Pennsylvania Railroad pointed out that in 1952, the railroad paid the city $324,000 in real estate taxes. Today, 12 years later, it is paying $1.8 million in taxes for the same property because of the improvements made on it.

In 1963, we turned the corner—the increase in tax ratables through urban renewal exceeded the assessments removed through redevelopment activity. From this point forward, we will enjoy the fruits of our undertakings in the continued increase in ratables, as a living demonstration of the validity of the whole concept of urban renewal. As a matter of fact, by 1969, the interval of our present six-year capital program, Philadelphia will have spent over a billion dollars in city and federal funds on urban renewal. In turn, a reasonable, yet conservative, estimate is that this will provide private investment and expansion well in excess of $5 billion.

There are a number of our planning principles and practices which I believe are worth reviewing, for they have made our work in downtown Philadelphia meaningful and productive and, above all, supportable by the business and banking fraternity and the community at large:

(1) Planning is economic. It is designed to retain business, trade and homes and to add new residential and commercial facilities. It is geared to conserve and build the supply of jobs and investment opportunities.

(2) It is practical. It is within the framework of our six-year capital program, adopted each year by the City Council—a schedule of what the city can afford with no increase in taxes. At the same time, through the carefully coordinated efforts of government and private enterprise, an amazing amount of the total work in downtown, as outlined in our comprehensive plan,

is already accomplished or under way and does not work to the prejudice of the total renewal activity.

(3) It is functional. The planning for downtown embraces a logical expression of regional considerations, particularly the regional transportation systems. Unified rail and bus terminal facilities will be constructed, and connections with the entire metropolitan region will be possible through coordinated regional efforts.

(4) It is culturally rich, respecting and enhancing historical landmarks and embellished by gardens and works of art. Our plans are built upon the original concept of William Penn, and they attempt to carry forward into our present day the clarity and simplicity of his idea for Philadelphia.

Finally, downtown must be attractive and exciting. Center city can survive only if people want to be there—if they can enjoy themselves, have fun and laugh, as well as earn a living and be inspired.

I say with some pride that the Philadelphia downtown story can certainly be told in terms of rates of investment, tax return, land planning and sound fiscal management. Not to be overlooked, however, are the importance of our concern for the view of a church spire, an architectural competition for a fountain on the Parkway, the comfort and convenience of commuters on a city-subsidized rail line, good restaurants and theater fare, the Philadelphia Orchestra, the quality of public and private education in downtown schools.

Above and beyond all else, we must never lose sight of the human factor in urban renewal—for the first ingredient in our cities is people.

It was not our vast national resources, the bricks and mortar, our technical and scientific competence, or whatever mastery we have achieved over the forces of nature which developed our cities and our nation.

It was—and it must be—people—people with vision who could, in an earlier day, draft a document such as the Declaration of Independence in the heart of Philadelphia, and, in a new day, dedicate themselves, their energies, their intelligence and their work to the city of the future. It is here that we find the initiative and imagination to make us willing to take the fire from the past and equally willing to leave the ashes. Nothing less than this kind of human dedication will do the job.

STATEMENT BY JOHN F. COLLINS, MAYOR OF BOSTON

I am sure I need not tell any of you of the critical importance of downtown to the life of an American city today—whether that city be a large metropolis or a small or medium-sized city. We should instead perhaps direct our attention toward informing Congress in particular and many other influential groups throughout the country of the need to expand and accelerate programs for downtown renewal.

American cities have been in the business of urban renewal for well over a decade. In that time, despite our best efforts, we have not witnessed any major breakthrough in the pattern and cycle of decay and obsolescence within the corporate limits of downtowns throughout America. Indeed, we have in many ways witnessed a worsening of the trends which we must reverse if our urban centers are to stay as healthy and prosperous as they should.

I refer first of all to the increasing transportation tangle—by no means limited to this fair city or to Boston or to Philadelphia or the other major urban centers. Secondly, the movement to suburbia, while perhaps healthy in many respects, has worked to surround our cities with prosperous enclaves while leaving within an increasing concentration of the poor and the elderly, the handicapped, as well as the minority groups struggling to find equal opportunities.

While this has occurred, the reliance on the property tax has, if anything, become more pronounced, which means in plain and simple terms that cities are expected to provide increasing and improved services on a regressive and outmoded tax basis.

Against this background, this accumulation of the neglect of the past thirty years, our successes in downtown renewal may seem small indeed. And yet, they do hold some promise if we are given adequate tools to finish the job.

A good start was made in the late Fifties when renewal regulations were liberalized to permit non-residential projects. These, I submit, are as vitally important to a city as are the necessary and very desirable neighborhood improvement and rehabilitation programs, for it is only with the assurance of increased jobs and productivity that a city has any hope at all of maintaining schools and community services, upon which the success of neighborhood improvement largely rests.

In Boston we have followed a partnership approach between the city administration and leading business interests in the downtown area. This approach, which is directly similar to our approach of having extensive consultation with neighborhood groups in residential projects, has produced results of which Boston can be proud and from which perhaps other cities can draw some useful lessons.

First of all, our giant Government Center Project, a combination of federal, state, and city offices together with major private office buildings and other private uses, will produce nearly $200 million in new construction and introduce more than 25,000 jobs into a handsome and well-located complex adjacent to our major retail area.

In the adjacent Waterfront Project an imaginative plan has been prepared, largely through the Chamber of Commerce, which will reclaim Boston's historic waterfront area as an exciting, attractive residential and commercial community. This project will generate more than $100 million in new, private construction.

Third, we have followed an approach of very direct cooperation in the preparation of an urban renewal plan for our downtown business district. In this case we have proceeded on the basis of full cooperation and joint financing of planning studies between the Redevelopment Authority and a specially-created Committee for the Central Business District. It is estimated that a sound renewal plan for Boston's central business district can generate up to $200 million in new construction and renovation.

These three projects spread over the major portion of the downtown Boston peninsula, while out in the Back Bay under a non-federally-assisted renewal project, the giant Prudential Center complex is now nearing completion. It represents an investment of well over $100 million with a new 52-story office building, a municipal auditorium and convention center, a 1,000-room hotel, and attractive shopping and recreation facilities.

This then is Boston's approach to downtown renewal. *First,* it is a comprehensive approach which seeks to treat all of the significant sections of downtown through a balanced and coordinated program. *Second,* it is a bold approach, and I suggest that the cities of America need, if anything, the support and encouragement to undertake bold—not timid—plans for the future. *Third,* our program rests heavily on the availability of federal financial assistance and the encouragement and leadership of the Administration in Washington.

We are not at all shy about this. Our cities contribute so heavily to the federal treasury and have such a limited framework of resources on their own that we must in all justice have the assurance of ample federal financial assistance.

This is not the most opportune time perhaps to speak optimistically about federal aid to help our cities rebuild. From all reports the 1964 Housing Act, which is desperately needed to replenish capital-grant funding authority, frankly speaking is in serious trouble. It needs the active support of concerned Mayors and civic leaders all across the country if it is to be passed. Without a housing bill this year, the urban renewal program will for all practical purposes shut down this summer.

Moreover, we need not only the housing bill, but as a top-priority item we must have the mass transit bill. This bill will help restore balance to our transportation system. Since 1956 we have poured hundreds and hundreds of millions of dollars into new expressways, while necessary transportation systems, including transit, rail, and bus, have been sadly neglected.

I am firmly an optimist by nature.

I regret to report that despite our successes in various cities around the country, we have as a nation not yet come to grips fully and completely with the need to reshape and rebuild our central cities. This year's legislative program is a must.

Beyond that—as always—the Mayors, civic leaders, and administrators in our cities must continue to provide the initiative and the leadership in seeing to it that America meets this challenge.

Statement by Wallace D. Henderson, Mayor of Fresno

If we didn't think cities are important, we wouldn't be here. However, Thomas Jefferson didn't think much of cities. He said they are "ulcers on the body politic." But others besides us have thought well of cities and have created great ones. Witness those of ancient Greece and Italy. Man's creative ability first expressed itself to its fullest extent when he began building a place to live.

Professor Eugene McQuillin says about cities: "The formation and everyday activities of centers of population have been the controlling important factor in the progress of mankind. The chief advances of human endeavor have been through the nurture and growth of urban life."

Certainly cities per se aren't necessarily good places to live. But people are gregarious and it's up to us to create good places to live. By good, I mean economically sound places, healthy places to dwell, aesthetic centers in which to live and bring up our children.

We in Fresno believe in our city. We decided not to let the downtown die. We were convinced that if this happened all good left in it would perish.

We found through an economic survey in 1958 that if we let our downtown core area deteriorate—and it was deteriorating—we would lose store after store. We learned that the central area in 1958 was attracting 18.6 percent of the trade sales in the six-county area of which Fresno is the hub in Central California.

Our economists told us that if deterioration went on, by 1980 the core area would have only 6.1 percent of the trade. Therefore, we knew we would have to perform radical surgery to save the downtown area. One of our leading merchants calls the resulting program the 3 R's—revolution, renaissance and revival.

Much tedious time went by before Fresno approached historic redevelopment events. A new City Council was born in 1958 which for the most part was made up of enthusiastic young men. We cooperated with businessmen who were trying to do something about revitalizing downtown. Another important factor was the help of the progressive McClatchy press—Fresno *Bee*—and, of course, the U.S. government. But even a start on such things as our mall complex didn't come overnight.

Finally, on April 1 this year the big bulldozers moved in like monstrous tanks into the main street in the heart of our city. At that moment those of us there to celebrate the occasion of the beginning of the mall had to admit—if only for a moment—that we had a few butterflies in our stomachs. Belief and faith were as much a part of what we were doing as statistics. But we felt better as the streets were ripped up. There was no turning back, and we were convinced that our new mall system would be completed by September 1 in time for the fall shopping season. In place of ugly black streets and sidewalks and automobiles there would be people, trees, fountains, pools and sculpture.

What were the main factors that allowed this change to take place? James H. J. Tate of Philadelphia is a Mayor who has had great success with a renewal program and he credits his great city's progress to four things: (1) Willingness to experiment with new techniques. (2) Comprehensive planning. (3) Enlightened participation by the entire community. (4) A firm faith in the future. These same four features are going into our successful renewal program. But we found they did not all fall into place easily, or at the same time. We had to win them.

We first had to find the techniques to use—techniques that would have a reasonable chance for success. Secondly, we had to take a second look midway in our downtown development to make our plan more comprehensive. Thirdly, we had to meet often, talk, argue and even bicker to bring about understanding with some of the opponents of the program.

The psychological resistance to change is always with us. Even at the present time we have those who make fun of the mall and belittle our efforts. "What a mess!" "Walking on dirt all over town." "Dust in the afternoon."

Others have more imagination and say with us that it will be beautiful. The majority are beginning to have a firm faith in the future of our city.

Early in 1958 we hired Victor Gruen and Associates for the overall planning for our downtown development. They proposed that we build malls in the center of the city. They said that only in this way could we recapture the dwindling tax base and the leadership of a six-county regional center. Furthermore, they said, we could stimulate Fresno aesthetically. After many hearings and more debate, we modified the original Gruen plan and called it the Fresno Plan. I would like to tell you briefly about the Fresno Plan.

It is a guide to the ultimate development of about 2,000 acres in the heart of Fresno. The boundary of the area is a street freeway system which will surround the triangle-shaped core. Even though the freeway loop system will not be completed for another ten years, the rest of the core area is developing rapidly with the construction of a new courthouse, convention center, federal building and Del Webb Hotel. That portion called the downtown occupies about 85 acres of the core area and this is the area in which the mall is located.

Today's downtown core area is located in 18 blocks, all separated by streets which make a grid pattern of intersections. The Fresno Plan eliminates the streets between these blocks and places a five-lane, one-way traffic loop as the boundary of this area. The result is a superblock tied together with the mall network.

Building the superblock involves widening boundary streets, building parking structures, selling cleared property for new business. The first step was installation of one-way streets in 1960. The widening project completed this spring was the second. The next will involve widening two more streets. Ultimately, diagonals will connect some of these streets. Soon after the loop is completed, two streets that have remained open across the mall will be closed and the loop will be the access to the system.

To have a successful mall you need good traffic flow and good parking. When our Fresno Plan is finished parking will increase from 2,500 to an estimated 7,400 spaces. It is predicted that the assessed value of land and buildings will increase from $8 million to $26 million.

Not only are we developing a mall with good traffic and good parking. We are making the mall aesthetically attractive. We have architectural control of the buildings. Furthermore, we are going to have 19 pieces of free-standing sculpture and we have raised over $150,000 by subscription from businessmen from all areas of the metropolis for them.

A new 3-R spirit has been born—the spirit of new Fresno. It has caught on because of this development and is affecting the city beneficially in every way. People throughout the United States are interested in investing in Fresno.

Our problem is to try to keep people going slowly enough to do things well enough to keep them from getting too far ahead of themselves. It is not like the spirit that was evidenced when a man appeared before our Council a few months ago and said: "If you would take the street cars out of downtown, we would have room to park." He didn't realize that the street cars had been out of the downtown area for 23 years. This man is an absentee landowner.

Today, people are shopping much more than they did before the streets were torn up. In fact, business has increased almost 10 per cent since the bulldozers started.

California was born with spirit. Now in 1964, as in 1849, we have it. It is a challenge to fight blight and decay in our cities. We in Fresno have accepted the challenge.

34 / HARLEM IS NOWHERE

A distinguished Negro novelist, Ralph Ellison, describes the tensions which have produced the personality of the inhabitant of the black ghettoes in the North. Compare Mr. Ellison's picture with the hopeful one of 1925 in Selection 13.

To live in Harlem is to dwell in the very bowels of the city; it is to pass a labyrinthine existence among streets that explode monotonously skyward with the spires and crosses of churches and clutter under foot with garbage and decay. Harlem is a ruin—many of its ordinary aspects (its crimes, its casual violence, its crumbling buildings with littered areaways, ill-smelling halls, and vermin-invaded rooms) are indistinguishable from the distorted images that appear in dreams, and which, like muggers haunting a lonely hall, quiver in the waking mind with hidden and threatening significance. Yet this is no dream but the reality of well over four hundred thousand Americans; a reality which for many defines and colors the world. Overcrowded and exploited politically and economically, Harlem is the scene and symbol of the Negro's perpetual alienation in the land of his birth.

But much has been written about the social and economic aspects of Harlem; I am here interested in its psychological character—a character that arises from the impact between urban slum conditions and folk sensibilities. Historically, American Negroes are caught in a vast process of change that has swept them from slavery to the condition of industrial man in

SOURCE: Ralph Ellison, *Shadow and Act* (New York: Random House, Inc., 1964).

a space of time so telescoped (a bare eighty-five years) that it is possible literally for them to step from feudalism into the vortex of industrialism simply by moving across the Mason-Dixon Line.

This abruptness of change and the resulting clash of cultural factors within Negro personality account for some of the extreme contrasts found in Harlem, for both its negative and its positive characteristics. For if Harlem is the scene of the folk-Negro's death agony, it is also the setting of his transcendence. Here it is possible for talented youths to leap through the development of decades in a brief twenty years, while beside them white-haired adults crawl in the feudal darkness of their childhood. Here a former cotton picker develops the sensitive hands of a surgeon, and men whose grandparents still believe in magic prepare optimistically to become atomic scientists. Here the grandchildren of those who possessed no written literature examine their lives through the eyes of Freud and Marx, Kierkegaard and Kafka, Malraux and Sartre. It explains the nature of a world so fluid and shifting that often within the mind the real and the unreal merge, and the marvelous beckons from behind the same sordid reality that denies its existence.

Hence the most surreal fantasies are acted out upon the streets of Harlem; a man ducks in and out of traffic shouting and throwing imaginary grenades that actually exploded during World War I; a boy participates in the rape-robbery of his mother; a man beating his wife in a park uses boxing "science" and observes Marquess of Queensberry rules (no rabbit punching, no blows beneath the belt); two men hold a third while a lesbian slashes him to death with a razor blade; boy gangsters wielding home-made pistols (which in the South of their origin are but toy symbols of adolescent yearning for manhood) shoot down their young rivals. Life becomes a masquerade, exotic costumes are worn every day. Those who cannot afford to hire a horse wear riding habits; others who could not afford a hunting trip or who seldom attend sporting events carry shooting sticks.

For this is a world in which the major energy of the imagination goes not into creating works of art, but to overcome the frustrations of social discrimination. Not quite citizens and yet

Americans, full of the tensions of modern man, but regarded as primitives, Negro Americans are in desperate search for an identity. Rejecting the second-class status assigned them, they feel alienated and their whole lives have become a search for answers to the questions: Who am I, What am I, Why am I, and Where? Significantly, in Harlem the reply to the greeting, "How are you?" is very often, "Oh, man, I'm *nowhere*"—a phrase revealing an attitude so common that it has been reduced to a gesture, a seemingly trivial word. Indeed, Negroes are not unaware that the conditions of their lives demand new definitions of terms like *primitive* and *modern, ethical* and *unethical, moral* and *immoral, patriotism* and *treason, tragedy* and *comedy, sanity* and *insanity*.

But for a long time now—despite songs like the "Blow Top Blues" and the eruption of expressions like *frantic, buggy,* and *mad* into Harlem's popular speech, doubtless a word-magic against the states they name—calm in face of the unreality of Negro life becomes increasingly difficult. And while some seek relief in strange hysterical forms of religion, in alcohol and drugs, others learn to analyze the causes for their predicament and join with others to correct them.

In relation to their Southern background, the cultural history of Negroes in the North reads like the legend of some tragic people out of mythology, a people which aspired to escape from its own unhappy homeland to the apparent peace of a distant mountain; but which, in migrating, made some fatal error of judgment and fell into a great chasm of mazelike passages that promise ever to lead to the mountain but end ever against a wall. Not that a Negro is worse off in the North than in the South, but that in the North he surrenders and does not replace certain important supports to his personality. He leaves a relatively static social order in which, having experienced its brutality for hundreds of years—indeed, having been formed within it and by it—he has developed those techniques of survival to which Faulkner refers as "endurance," and an ease of movement within explosive situations which makes Hemingway's definition of courage, "grace under pressure," appear mere swagger. He surrenders the protection of his peasant cynicism—his refusal to hope for the fulfillment of hopeless hopes—and his sense of being "at home in the world" gained from confronting and accepting (for day-to-day living, at least) the obscene absurdity of his predicament. Further, he leaves a still authoritative religion which gives his life a semblance of metaphysical wholeness; a family structure which is relatively stable; and a body of folklore—tested in life-and-death terms against his daily experience with nature and the Southern white man—that serves him as a guide to action.

These are the supports of Southern Negro rationality (and, to an extent, of the internal peace of the United States); humble, but of inestimable psychological value,* they allow Southern Negroes to maintain their almost mystical hope for a future of full democracy—a hope accompanied by an irrepressible belief in some Mecca of equality, located in the North and identified by the magic place names New York, Chicago, Detroit. A belief sustained (as all myth is sustained by ritual) by identifying themselves ritually with the successes of Negro celebrities, by reciting their exploits and enumerating their dollars, and by recounting the swiftness with which they spiral from humble birth to headline fame. And doubtless the blasting of this dream is as damaging to Negro personality as the slum scenes of filth, disorder, and crumbling masonry in which it flies apart.

When Negroes are barred from participating in the main institutional life of society, they lose far more than economic privileges or the satisfaction of saluting the flag with unmixed emotions. They lose one of the bulwarks which men place between themselves and the constant threat of chaos. For whatever the assigned function of social institutions, their psychological function is to protect the citizen against the irrational, incalculable forces that hover about the edges of human life like cosmic destruction lurking within an atomic stockpile.

* Their political and economic value is the measure of both the positive and negative characteristics of American democracy.

And it is precisely the denial of this support through segregation and discrimination that leaves the most balanced Negro open to anxiety.

Though caught not only in the tensions arising from his own swift history, but in those conflicts created in modern man by a revolutionary world, he cannot participate fully in the therapy which the white American achieves through patriotic ceremonies and by identifying himself with American wealth and power. Instead, he is thrown back upon his own "slum-shocked" institutions.

But these, like his folk personality, are caught in a process of chaotic change. His family disintegrates, his church splinters; his folk wisdom is discarded in the mistaken notion that it in no way applies to urban living; and his formal education (never really his own) provides him with neither scientific description nor rounded philosophical interpretation of the profound forces that are transforming his total being. Yet even his art is transformed; the lyrical ritual elements of folk jazz—that artistic projection of the only real individuality possible for him in the South, that embodiment of a superior democracy in which each individual cultivated his uniqueness and yet did not clash with his neighbors—have given way to the near-themeless technical virtuosity of bebop, a further triumph of technology over humanism. His speech hardens; his movements are geared to the time clock; his diet changes; his sensibilities quicken; and his intelligence expands. But without institutions to give him direction, and lacking a clear explanation of his predicament—the religious ones being inadequate, and those offered by political and labor leaders obviously incomplete and opportunistic—the individual feels that his world and his personality are out of key. The phrase "I'm nowhere" expresses the feeling borne in upon many Negroes that they have no stable, recognized place in society. One's identity drifts in a capricious reality in which even the most commonly held assumptions are questionable. One "is" literally, but one is nowhere; one wanders dazed in a ghetto maze, a "displaced person" of American democracy.

And as though all this were not enough of a strain on a

people's sense of the rational, the conditions under which it lives are seized upon as proof of its inferiority. Thus the frustrations of Negro life (many of them the frustrations of *all* life during this historical moment) permeate the atmosphere of Harlem with a hostility that bombards the individual from so many directions that he is often unable to identify it with any specific object. Some feel it the punishment of some racial or personal guilt and pray to God; others (called "evil Negroes" in Harlem) become enraged with the world. Sometimes it provokes dramatic mass responses.

And why have these explosive matters—which are now a problem of our foreign policy—been ignored? Because there is an argument in progress between black men and white men as to the true nature of American reality. Following their own interests, whites impose interpretations upon Negro experience that are not only false but, in effect, a denial of Negro humanity. Too weak to shout down these interpretations, Negroes live nevertheless as they have to live, and the concrete conditions of their lives are more real than white men's arguments.

35 / THE SEARCH FOR QUALITY IN OUR CITIES

The dean of Tulane University's School of Architecture, John W. Lawrence, pleads for beauty and excellence in America's cities, urging, as a vital beginning, that his city halt the erosion of its colorful landmarks by commercial greed.

In the Soviet Union there is maximum capability for taking advantage of the techniques of planning, but this has not resulted in the creation of beautiful and humane cities. In the United States of America there is unparalleled affluence—money to make cities—but this also has not created beautiful cities.

It is a stand-off. The one who finds the way or ways to mate technique and means will do mankind a far greater service than that promised by the first moon landing. For, in finding this way, the salvation of man's sanity may be the reward.

In our affluent society not one in a hundred, given the means of time and money, is able to surround himself with grace and beauty.

We have not, as before, a way to build, but instead, an infinity of ways, out of which only the most talented can identify the meaningful. The discipline of poverty is gone; and so with it, the incapability of pre-industrial society for artistic error. In describing man's traditional needs for food, clothing and shelter in the Affluent Society, J. K. Galbraith says that in the United States, more die from over-eating than from starvation; our clothing is almost totally responsive to erotic considerations, and

SOURCE: John W. Lawrence, "Address to the Board of Directors, Urban America, Inc., New Orleans, La., May 16, 1966." Reprinted by permission.

we tear down perfectly good buildings to make way for bad ones.

Let this stand insufficiently as a description of our world as we now undertake for a moment an all-too-brief look at New Orleans.

It is not an easy task, I think you will agree, to come before you and try in ten minutes to tell you something of this city—its rich fabric of inheritance now assailed from all directions, its hopes and its ideals, its frustrations, and most importantly to me, and I think, to you, its scale of values.

Had I been given this task a few months ago, it would have been even more difficult; for during these past months a few encouraging events have taken place and it is proper that I should mention these first in this moment of self-analysis.

We have sent to our State Legislature the best delegation ever to represent this City.

There is much agreement too that the newly installed City Council is the best we have ever had and we hope for much from them.

The electorate has just passed by a very convincing margin an additional one percent sales tax for the support of our public schools desperately needed. Several previous efforts had failed.

The United Fund as well as the Cultural Attractions Fund have both surpassed their goals this year.

There is underway a Community Renewal program grant—one of the most important planning surveys ever undertaken here, by which we hope to discover more about who and what we are.

We are among the least geographically segregated communities in the United States.

You have just heard from Mr. Marcou of the unique study of the Vieux Carre which his firm is making under the sponsorship of the Bureau of Governmental Research.

While this list is not exhaustive, it will serve to indicate quite clearly that all in New Orleans is not bad. Were I to stop here, as many spokesmen for New Orleans do, you might conclude that we are a model of civic enterprise, virtue and accomplishment.

But your eyes and your senses and your instincts tell you otherwise.

In terms of environmental issues we are an almost totally uninformed community. The people at large have no notion of the degree of our relative insolvency here, because nobody will tell them—neither their representatives nor the press, and those few who will, have no voice for the dissemination of their views.

Only the efforts of a private Citizen's Housing Council and the Catholic weekly—*The Clarion Herald*—seem to have forged an official concern for housing blight which has few, if any, equals for a community this size in the United States. It is our scandal and our shame.

Should it be necessary to remind us that after six years or more the Greater New Orleans Expressway has not had one tree planted on its course, only endless ranges of chain link fence?

The entrances to our city are a disgrace—something to despoil the spirit and cause one to die a little every time they are traversed. Those of you who came by plane know that no civilization in history has ever created anything so ugly as the drive from New Orleans airport to the Central Business District. That men could wreak such vulgarity upon their neighbors with the full support of law is both shocking and prophetic of decline.

At the eastern entrance to the city, the hypnotizing endlessness of galvanized poles of fearful scale begets not a murmur from press or official spokesmen.

Is there no one to speak for the right of every citizen to be free from the intrusion of billboard blight on every hand? At least you can turn television off. When the advertising interests and their lobbies completely abandon their responsibility as they jar and shatter the landscape, with the citizen helpless against the assault, then obviously legislation is needed.

The broadening of the police power concept of government to include aesthetics as well as health, safety and morals is now well-established in American jurisprudence.

Some of you may not know that Louisiana is the only state that prohibits Urban Renewal by legislative act. Yet Urban

Renewal will and must come to this city as surely as darkness will follow the sun's decline. Many here and elsewhere in authority in the city know this, yet the voice is yet to arise which seeks to delineate this necessity to the Community.

A poll taken recently by the *Clarion-Herald* shows conclusively that the people of this community recognize the need for Urban Renewal. It is essential that the City Planning Commission develop an Urban Renewal Planning capability before it is beset with the need for crisis planning.

In the collision between the twentieth century and the nineteenth, New Orleans has been faring badly. The Vieux Carre is beleaguered as never before. Armed with sophisticated legislation since 1937, the Quarter nonetheless is succumbing to predatory influences that will be its undoing—a kind of hit and run assault—which shrewdly recognizes that outer appearances of the remaining authentic will hold up at least until the new ersatz is amortized. Then the predators can pick up their marbles and go elsewhere.

The simple fact that an undistinguished building that belongs in the Quarter and helped make it what it is, is infinitely superior to a phony in "official" style, seems to go totally undetected. Far better would it be on the most grave occasions of necessity to build excellent contemporary buildings. At least this would be consistent with the vigorous tradition of the Quarter. The caricatures do not preserve, nor can they be called architecture or archaeology. Like many caricatures they hold within them the seeds of impending tragedy.

But the mood of the city is such that this nonsense is condoned, even applauded. The Quarter is whittled away by greedy buildings, its delicate balance distorted, while one bad building after another is welcomed as a statistic for an annual summary, and in New Orleans now anything that can't be put in a column of figures doesn't exist, notwithstanding the peculiar inability of statistics to measure quality. And so it goes. The charm of authentic background building—the tout ensemble—is being eroded away by an arrogant proliferation of Hollywood foreground buildings. One could hardly imagine that the Vieux Carre legislation was enacted to "preserve the quaint and distinctive historic and architectural character" of the area.

. . . . .

The mood which I have tried to describe—one honoring ideas only originating from a mercantile thrust—is essentially a mood of rampant anti-intellectualism. It is a mood which exalts the philosophy "if you're so smart, why ain't you rich?" It is a mood which dramatizes the growing breach between the individual and collective interests. It is finally a mood of rugged individualism with the failure to recognize, however, that there is no longer a frontier to which we may retreat and leave our sins behind.

If New Orleans is to regain in the twentieth century the place in human affairs and dignity which it held in the nineteenth century, it must consciously re-dedicate itself to quality and excellence—commodities which have persistently eluded the city in most aspects of its building. It must earnestly seek answers to why what is happening in Boston, Toronto, Philadelphia, is not happening here. To fail to do this much is to recognize that events have outrun the ability of the Establishment to deal with them in terms of concept or technique.

36 / THE CITY COMES INTO ITS OWN

President Lyndon B. Johnson appeals to the Congress to launch a national effort to make the cities livable. These paragraphs are from his successful request for the establishment of a Cabinet Department of Housing and Urban Development.

Throughout man's history, the city has been at the center of civilization. It is at the center of our own society. Over 70 percent of our population—135 million Americans—live in urban areas. A half century from now 320 million of our 400 million Americans will live in such areas. And our largest cities will receive the greatest impact of growth.

Numbers alone do not make this an urban nation. Finance and culture, commerce, and government make their home in the city and draw their vitality from it. Within the borders of our urban centers can be found the most impressive achievements of man's skill and the highest expressions of man's spirit, as well as the worst examples of degradation and cruelty and misery to be found in modern America.

The city is not an assembly of shops and buildings. It is not a collection of goods and services. It is a community for the enrichment of the life of man. It is a place for the satisfaction of man's most urgent needs and his highest aspirations. It is an instrument for the advance of civilization. Our task is to put the highest concerns of our people at the center of urban growth and activity. It is to create and preserve the sense of community with

SOURCE: Lyndon B. Johnson, "Message on Cities—Message from the President of the United States." H. Doc. No. 99, *Congressional Record,* 89th Cong., 1st Sess. (March 2, 1965), Vol. III, Pt. 3, pp. 3908–12.

others which gives us significance and security, a sense of belonging and of sharing in the common life.

Aristotle said: "Men come together in cities in order to live. They remain together in order to live the good life."

The modern city can be the most ruthless enemy of the good life, or it can be its servant. The choice is up to this generation of Americans. For this is truly the time of decision for the American city.

In our time, two giant and dangerous forces are converging on our cities: the forces of growth and decay.

Between today and the year 2000, more than 80 percent of our population increase will occur in urban areas. During the next 15 years, 30 million people will be added to our cities—equivalent to the combined population of New York, Chicago, Los Angeles, Philadelphia, Detroit, and Baltimore. Each year, in the coming generation, we will add the equivalent of 15 cities of 200,000 each.

Already old cities are tending to combine into huge clusters. The strip of land from southern New Hampshire to northern Virginia contains 21 percent of America's population in 1.8 percent of its areas. Along the west coast, the Great Lakes, and the Gulf of Mexico, other urban giants are merging and growing.

Our new city dwellers will need homes and schools and public services. By 1975 we will need over 2 million new homes a year. We will need schools for 10 million additional children, welfare and health facilities for 5 million more people over the age of 60, transportation facilities for the daily movement of 200 million people and more than 80 million automobiles.

In the remainder of this century—in less than 40 years—urban population will double, city land will double, and we will have to build in our cities as much as all that we have built since the first colonist arrived on these shores. It is as if we had 40 years to rebuild the entire urban United States.

Yet these new overwhelming pressures are being visited upon cities already in distress. We have over 9 million homes, most of them in cities, which are run down or deteriorating; over 4 million do not have running water or even plumbing. Many of our central cities are in need of major surgery to overcome decay. New suburban sprawl reaches out into the countryside, as the process of urbanization consumes a million acres a year. The old, the poor, the discriminated against are increasingly concentrated in central city ghettos; while others move to the suburbs leaving the central city to battle against immense odds.

Physical decay, from obsolescent schools to polluted water and air, helps breed social decay. It casts a pall of ugliness and despair on the spirits of the people. And this is reflected in rising crime rates, school dropouts, delinquency and social disorganization.

Our cities are making a valiant effort to combat the mounting dangers to the good life. Between 1954 and 1963 per capita municipal tax revenues increased by 43 percent, and local government indebtedness increased by 119 percent. City officials with inadequate resources, limited authority, too few trained people, and often with too little public support, have, in many cases, waged a heroic battle to improve the life of the people they serve.

But we must do far more as a nation if we are to deal effectively with one of the most critical domestic problems of the United States.

Let us be clear about the core of this problem. The problem is people and the quality of the lives they lead. We want to build not just housing units, but neighborhoods; not just to construct schools, but to educate children; not just to raise income, but to create beauty and end the poisoning of our environment. We must extend the range of choices available to all our people so that all, and not just the fortunate, can have access to decent homes and schools, to recreation and to culture. We must work to overcome the forces which divide our people and erode the vitality which comes from the partnership of those with diverse incomes and interests and backgrounds.

The problems of the city are problems of housing and education. They involve increasing employment and ending poverty. They call for beauty and nature, recreation, and an end to racial discrimination. They are, in large measure, the problems of

American society itself. They call for a generosity of vision, a breadth of approach, a magnitude of effort which we have not yet brought to bear on the American city.

Whatever the scale of its programs, the Federal Government will only be able to do a small part of what is required. The vast bulk of resources and energy, of talent and toil, will have to come from State and local governments, private interests, and individual citizens. But the Federal Government does have a responsibility. It must help to meet the most urgent national needs; in housing, in education, in health, and many other areas. It must also be sure that its efforts serve as a catalyst and as a lever to help and guide State and local governments toward meeting their problems.

We must also recognize that this message, and the program it proposes, does not fully meet the problems of the city. In part, this is because many other programs, such as those for education and health, are dealt with separately. But it is also because we do not have all the answers. In the last few years there has been an enormous growth of interest and knowledge and intellectual ferment. We need more thought and wisdom and knowledge as we painfully struggle to identify the ills, the dangers, and the cures for the American city. We need to reshape, at every level of government, our approach to problems which are often different than we thought and larger than we had imagined.

I want to begin that process today.

We begin with the awareness that the city, possessed of its own inexorable vitality, has ignored the classic jurisdictions of municipalities and counties and States. The organic unit we call the city spreads across the countryside, enveloping towns, building vast new suburbs, destroying trees and streams. Access to suburbs has changed the character of the central city. The jobs and income of suburbanites may depend upon the opportunities for work and learning offered by the central city. Polluted air and water do not respect the jurisdictions of mayors and city councils or even of Governors. Wealthy suburbs often form an enclave whereby the well-to-do and the talented can escape from the problems of their neighbors, thus impoverishing the ability of the city to deal with its problems.

The interests and needs of many of the communities which make up the modern city often seem to be in conflict. But they all have an overriding interest in improving the quality of life of their people. And they have an overriding interest in enriching the quality of American civilization. These interests will only be served by looking at the metropolitan area as a whole, and planning and working for its development.

. . . . .

Many of these programs are intended to help the poor and those stripped of opportunity. But our goal is more ambitious than that. It is nothing less than to improve the quality of life for every American. In this quest the future of the American city will play the most vital role. There are a few whose affluence enables them to move through the city guarded and masked from the realities of the life around them. But they are few indeed. For the rest of us the quality and condition of our lives is inexorably fixed by the nature of the community in which we live. Slums and ugliness, crime and congestion, growth and decay inevitably touch the life of all. Those who would like to enjoy the lovely parks of some of our great cities soon realize that neither wealth nor position fully protects them against the failures of society. Even among strangers, we are neighbors.

We are still only groping toward solution. The next decade should be a time of experimentation. Our cities will not settle into a drab uniformity directed from a single center. Each will choose its own course of development—whether it is to unite communities or build entirely new metropolitan areas. We will seek new ways to structure our suburbs and our transportation; new techniques for introducing beauty and improving homes. This is an effort which must command the most talented and trained of our people and call upon administrators and officials to act with generosity of vision and spaciousness of imagination.

I believe today's proposals are an important start along that road. They should help us to look upon the city as it really is: a vast and myriad complex of homes and communities, people and their needs, hopes and frustrations. It can liberate the expectations of men, or it can crush them in body and spirit.

For underneath all the rest, at the very bottom of all we do, is the effort to protect, under the conditions of the modern world, values as old as this Nation and the civilization from which it comes. We work in our cities to satisfy our needs for shelter and work and the ability to command a satisfying way of life. We wish to create a city where men and women can feed the hunger of the spirit for beauty and have access to the best of man's work; where education and the richness of diversity expands our horizons and extends our expectations. But we also look for something more.

The American city should be a collection of communities where every member has a right to belong. It should be a place where every man feels safe on his streets and in the house of his friends. It should be a place where each individual's dignity and self-respect is strengthened by the respect and affection of his neighbors. It should be a place where each of us can find the satisfaction and warmth which comes only from being a member of the community of man. This is what man sought at the dawn of civilization. It is what we seek today.